GAY AND LESBIAN WRITERS

Oscar Wilde

GAY AND LESBIAN WRITERS

James Baldwin
Allen Ginsberg
Adrienne Rich
Sappho
Walt Whitman
Oscar Wilde

GAY AND LESBIAN WRITERS

Oscar Wilde

Jeff Nunokawa and Amy Sickels

Lesléa Newman
Series Editor

CHELSEA HOUSE
PUBLISHERS

A Haights Cross Communications ✦ Company ®

Philadelphia

CHELSEA HOUSE PUBLISHERS

VP, NEW PRODUCT DEVELOPMENT Sally Cheney
DIRECTOR OF PRODUCTION Kim Shinners
CREATIVE MANAGER Takeshi Takahashi
MANUFACTURING MANAGER Diann Grasse

Staff for OSCAR WILDE

EXECUTIVE EDITOR: Matt Uhler
EDITORIAL ASSISTANT: Sarah Sharpless
PHOTO EDITOR: Sarah Bloom
SERIES AND COVER DESIGNER: Takeshi Takahashi
LAYOUT: EJB Publishing Services

 A Haights Cross Communications Company ®

http://www.chelseahouse.com

First Printing

9 8 7 6 5 4 3 2 1

Library of Congress Cataloging-in-Publication Data
Nunokawa, Jeff, 1958-
  Oscar Wilde / Jeff Nunokawa and Amy Sickels.
    p. cm. — (Gay and lesbian writers)
  Includes index.
  ISBN 0-7910-8219-9 (alk. paper) — ISBN 0-7910-8388-8 (pbk.) 1.
Wilde, Oscar, 1854-1900. 2. Authors, Irish—19th century—Biography. 3.
Gay men—Great Britain—Biography. I. Sickels, Amy. II. Title. III. Series.
  PR5823.N86 2005
  828'.809—dc22
                              2005004020

Cover: Library of Congress, LC-USZ62-25533

TABLE OF CONTENTS

PRIDE

MANY YEARS AGO, IN 1970 to be exact, I began my career as a high school student. Those were the dark ages, before cell phones and CD players, before computers and cable TV, before the words "gay" and "pride" ever—at least to my knowledge— appeared in the same sentence. In fact, I remember the very first time I saw the word "gay" appear in a newspaper. It was in the early 1970s, a year after the 1969 Stonewall riots when a group of butches and drag queens fought back against a police raid on a gay bar, sparking what was then known as the "gay liberation movement." I was sitting in our Long Island living room with my brothers, my parents, and some visiting relatives. One of the adults picked up the newspaper, read a headline about the anniversary of Stonewall and said in a voice dripping with disapproval, "Well, all I can say is *gay* certainly meant something different in my time." There were a few murmurs of agreement, and then the matter was dropped. I learned very quickly that this subject was taboo in the Newman household.

Not that I had any inkling that I would grow up to be a lesbian. All I knew was that I didn't want to get married and have children, I wasn't interested in boys, and all I wanted to do was read books, write poetry, and spend time with my best friend, Vicki, who lived three houses away. My friendship with Vicki was strictly platonic, but even so, taunts of "Leslie the lezzie, Leslie the lezzie" followed me up and down the hallways of

Jericho High School. (I changed my name from Leslie to Lesléa when I was sixteen largely because, due to my gender-free name, I was, much to my horror, enrolled in the boys' gym class.)

Interestingly enough, Vicki was never once teased for being a lesbian; did my classmates know something I didn't know?

In 1973 I left home to attend the University of Vermont. There was no gay/straight alliance on campus, nor were there courses in gay literature or gay history. Though I studied the poetry of Gertrude Stein, I was never led to believe that Alice B. Toklas was anything more than the poet's housekeeper and cook. Though I studied Walt Whitman's work and read the novels of James Baldwin, there was never any mention of either man's sexuality. And even though I still was unaware of my own sexuality, I knew somehow that I was "different." I did not want the same things most of the young women around me wanted, namely a husband and children. I did not know being a lesbian was a possibility. Since I wasn't interested in boys "that way," I simply thought I was not a sexual being.

What saved me was the Beat movement, and specifically the Beat poets: Allen Ginsberg, Peter Orlovsky, Gary Snyder, Anne Waldman, and Ted Berrigan, all of whom became my teachers when I hitchhiked out to Boulder, Colorado, and enrolled in Naropa Institute's Jack Kerouac School of Disembodied Poetics. The Beats were unabashedly sexual. Allen and Peter were clearly a couple; there was also a pair of lesbians on the faculty who made no secret of the fact that they lived together. I learned about Sappho and the island of Lesbos; I learned that Virginia Woolf and Vita Sackville-West were not merely pen pals; I learned that Emily Dickinson had a correspondence with her sister-in-law Susan Huntington Dickinson that some interpreted as romantic. And though these women may or may not have been lesbians, the discovery that women could be primary in each other's lives in a passionate way filled me with a sense of excitement and hope. Finally I realized that I wasn't a freak. There were others like me. A world of possibilities opened up before my eyes.

In 1999, I was invited back to my alma mater to be inducted into the Jericho High School Hall of Fame. The world had changed in many ways since I graduated in 1973. The words "gay" and "lesbian" now appeared in many newspapers across the country on a regular basis, and the gay, lesbian, bisexual, and transgendered community even had its own newspapers and magazines. In 1977, Harvey Milk, the first openly out politician in this country, had been elected as a San Francisco City Supervisor (tragically he was assasinated in his office the following year). Most large cities had gay and lesbian pride parades during the month of June and many high schools had gay straight alliances (Concord High School in Concord, Massachusetts started the first GSA in 1989). The "gayby boom" had begun as more and more lesbians and gay men were starting families, and the gay marriage movement was going strong.

Since graduating from high school, my life had changed dramatically as well. In 1988 I met the woman of my dreams and a year later, on September 10, 1989, we celebrated our relationship with a lifetime commitment ceremony (On September 10, 2004, we renewed our vows before a justice of the peace, making our fifteen-year marriage legal in the state of Massachusetts). I had published close to thirty books, most of which had gay or lesbian content, including the picture book, *Heather Has Two Mommies*, which became one of the most controversial and challenged books of the 1990s. And I had become a political activist, speaking out for the rights of lesbians and gay men every chance I could.

When I was inducted into Jericho High School's Hall of Fame, I was invited to come to campus to give a speech at a school assembly. It was only upon arrival that I was informed that the students knew only one thing about me: I was an author. They did not know the titles of my books and they did not know I was a lesbian. Consequently, I had the unexpected opportunity to come out to an entire high school population. If the students were surprised, they did not show it. Jericho students are nothing if not polite. But they did ask interesting questions. They wanted to know if I had dated boys when I was in high school (yes); they wanted to know how old I was when I came out (twenty-seven); they wanted to know if I wished that I were straight (no, but sometimes I wish my hair was). At one point the questions came to a halt, so I decided to ask my audience, "What is it like for gay and lesbian students today at Jericho High School?" The auditorium was quiet for a moment and then a boy called out, "We don't have any gay students."

About a year later, I received an email from a Jericho High School alumna who graduated in June of 1999. She told me she was a lesbian and had known so since she was fifteen years old. She had been at my induction assembly, but did not feel comfortable coming out in front of her peers that day, or even privately to me. Only after she graduated from high school and went away to college did she feel safe enough to be out. Clearly many things had changed since I'd attended Jericho High School and many things had not.

A book is a powerful thing, and literature can change people's lives. If I had read a biography about a lesbian writer when I was in high school, I truly believe my life would have been vastly different. I might very well have been spared years of pain and confusion because I would have known that a life very much like the one I am now living is possible. If the books in this series had been on the Jericho High School curriculum in 1999, perhaps the young woman who sent me an email would have felt safe enough to come out of the closet before graduation.

It is my hope that this book and others like it will help high school students know that not everyone is heterosexual, and that gay, lesbian, bisexual, and transgendered people can and do live happy, productive, inspiring, and creative lives. The writers included in this series have certainly left their mark on society with their award-winning works of poetry and prose. May they inspire us all to be exactly who we are with pride and celebration.

—Lesléa Newman, 2004

INTRODUCTION

WILD ABOUT OSCAR

Every time I visit New York, I get caught up in the fast pace and hustle-bustle of the most exciting city in the world. There's always something new to see and do, yet no matter how busy I am, I always make time to visit a place I have been to countless times before. It is an elegant brick building located at 15 Christopher Street in the West Village, a neighborhood known for its large gay population. I trot up the steps, pull open the door and step inside a small bookshop that sells literature of interest to the gay, lesbian, bisexual, and transgendered community. In 1967 when the store opened a few blocks away at its original location, it was the only gay bookstore in the entire world and it quickly became known as a place to gather and hold meetings for cultural and political activities. This landmark bookstore which moved to its present site in 1973 is often the first place out-of-towners visit as they arrive in New York, searching for the "gay scene."

The name of this establishment is the Oscar Wilde Bookshop.

During his lifetime, the mere mention of Oscar Wilde's name could send other homosexual men into a terrified silence. And now his name is emblazoned on a plaque outside a gay bookstore for all the world to see.

I call this poetic justice.

I like to think Oscar Wilde would feel delighted and deserving of such an honor, after all, he was quite fond of himself. He once said, "To love oneself is the beginning of a lifelong romance." Perhaps if he were alive, he would climb the stoop at 15 Christopher Street, pull open the door, step inside and start to browse. Maybe he'd head over to the memoir section, since he once said, "My own business bores me to death. I prefer other people's." Or perhaps he would leave the store empty-handed, since he also said, "I never travel without my diary. One should always have something sensational to read on the train." Whether he bought a book or not, I'm sure Oscar Wilde would be astounded at the number of volumes available for his perusal and purchase. I don't imagine the idea of such a bookstore was conceivable during his lifetime.

As Jeff Nunokawa and Amy Sickels' fascinating biography will tell you, Oscar Fingal O'Flahertie Wills Wilde was born in 1854 and died in 1900. During his short life he was famous and infamous, revered and reviled. He was a playwright, a poet, a critic, an essayist, a novelist, and a great wit. He was also a homosexual in a time when that was simply unacceptable. During the Victorian era, having same-sex relationships was a crime considered so horrendous, same-sex romance became known as "the love that dare not speak its name."

Yet Oscar Wilde dared to live his life the way he wanted to, despite the consequences. When he fell in love with Lord Alfred Douglas, he did not keep their relationship a secret. And when given the chance to flee England and escape prosecution on indecent acts charges, he chose to stay. For the crime of loving another man, he was prosecuted, convicted and sentenced to two years of hard labor.

When Justice Wills sentenced Oscar Wilde in 1895, he said, "It is no use for me to address you. People who can do these things must be dead to all sense of shame and one cannot hope to produce any effect upon them. It is the worst case I have ever tried." When I read those words, my first response was, "Well, that was more than one-hundred years ago. Thank God, times have changed." But then I remembered something.

In February of 2002, a custody case involving a lesbian mother, her former husband, and their three children was tried by the Alabama State Supreme Court. The court ruled against the children's mother, and Judge Roy Moore stated, "Homosexual conduct is, and has been, considered abhorrent, immoral, detestable, a crime against nature, and a violation of the laws of nature and of nature's God upon which this Nation and our laws are predicated."

Despite the fact that times have changed in many ways—the "love that dare not speak its name" is now mentioned in newspapers and magazines and on radio and television on a daily basis all over the world—there are many ways in which times have not changed at all.

Still we go on, living our lives and fighting for what we know is right. And even though Oscar Wilde's life ended in tragedy—he died at age 46, three years after he was released from prison—we can be inspired by his courage. Oscar Wilde refused to obey the rules and regulations of a society he found extremely oppressive. He would not dress the way that he was expected to dress, he would not act the way that he was expected to act, and he would not love the way he was expected to love. Oscar Wilde was first and foremost always entirely himself. And though he is no longer among us, he has triumphed by achieving a writer's best revenge. Shortly after his arrest, his name was dropped from the programs of his plays; soon after that, production of plays he had written was suspended altogether. But now, more than a hundred years after his death, Oscar Wilde's work lives on, and his plays, most notably, "The Importance of Being Ernest" are performed in high school auditoriums, community playhouses and professional theatres regularly and to great acclaim.

The last time I visited New York City, I made my way down Christopher Street and stepped into the Oscar Wilde Bookshop. The store manager greeted me by name, I autographed copies of my books, and bought a poetry collection and several magazines. Darkness had fallen by the time I left the store. As I stepped out onto the street and looked up at a clear, brilliant sky, I remembered the words of Oscar Wilde: "All of us are in the gutter, but some of us are looking up at the stars." I looked from the sky to the plaque bearing the name of Oscar Wilde. A rainbow flag hanging next to it fluttered in the breeze. As I stood there, two young gay men holding hands and laughing as though they hadn't a care in the world walked by me and headed into the bookshop. I like to think Oscar Wilde, somewhere up among the stars, looked down and smiled.

Death by Shame

The best thing for everybody now is to forget all about Oscar Wilde, his perpetual posings, his aesthetical teachings and his theatrical productions. Let him go into silence, and be heard no more.

—The Echo

ON MAY 25, 1895, IN THE LONDON court called Old Bailey, two men were condemned for the "unspeakable crime" of sexual intercourse with other men. While two men were charged, the crowds that had gathered to hear the verdict were really only interested in one of them. Alfred Taylor was merely an upper-class boy gone wrong: his conviction was lost in the international uproar that arose when he and his codefendant were sentenced to two years of hard labor for a crime that English law called so horrible that it could not even be mentioned by Christians ("peccatum illud horribile, inter christonos non nominandum").

For Taylor shared the defendant's bench with one of the most illustrious men in the Western world. "Somehow or another," Oscar Wilde had vowed to his classmates at Oxford, "I'll be famous, and if not famous, notorious," and by the time of his conviction, Wilde had more than kept his promise: he had written some of the most successful plays of the 19th century; he was the most influential critic of the late Victorian era; he dominated the world of fashion, decoration, and art as a speaker, editor, and polemicist; his fairy tales, stories, and poetry amused, delighted, and instructed vast audiences in Europe and the United States; his witty paradoxes were heard and repeated around the world. Playwright, Essayist, Novelist, Poet, Epigrammatist, Fashion Czar, Lord of High Society, and Idiosyncratic Socialist, Oscar Wilde was still more than the sum of his parts: his gigantic personality was expansive enough to serve as the emblem of his era.

A hush fell over the courtroom when Mr. Justice Wills turned to sentence the man thought by many to be the cleverest person in the world. Thirty-five years later, the courtroom drama of Wilde's ruin was still fresh in the mind of one who had witnessed it: "I have seen many awful happenings at the Old Bailey, but to me no death sentence has ever seemed so terrible as the one which Mr. Justice Wills delivered when his duty called upon him to destroy and take from the world the man who had given it so much." No one who heard Mr. Justice Wills that day would be inclined to dispute this account; a one-man Terror, his remarks to the prisoners were like the bullets of a firing squad:

> Oscar Wilde and Alfred Taylor, the crime of which you have been convicted is so bad that one has to put stern restraint on oneself to prevent oneself from describing, in language I would rather not use, the sentiments which must rise to the breast of every man of honour who has heard the details of these two terrible trials. That the jury have arrived at a correct verdict in this case I cannot persuade myself to entertain the shadow of a doubt; and I hope, at all events that those who sometimes imagine that a judge is half-hearted in the cause of decency and morality because he takes care no prejudice shall enter into the case, may see that that is consistent at least with a common sense of indignation at the horrible charges brought home to both of you.
>
> It is no use for me to address you. People who can do these things must be dead to all sense of shame, and one cannot hope to produce any effect upon them. It is the worst case I have ever tried. That you, Taylor, kept a kind of male brothel it is impossible to doubt. And that you, Wilde, have been the centre of a circle of extensive corruption of the most hideous kind among young men, it is equally impossible to doubt.
>
> I shall, under such circumstances, be expected to pass the severest sentence that the law allows. In my judgement it is totally inadequate for such a case as this. The sentence of the Court is that each of you be imprisoned and kept to hard labour for two years.

Some gasps of shock and cries of "Shame" were heard; the violence of the judge's remarks were unexpected to many, and, to a few, seemed unjust. But these lonely protests were soon crowded aside by the cheers that arose in the courtroom, and beyond. Inside, spectators shouted for joy; outside, crowds danced in the streets. Wilde's faint voice was briefly heard as he sought to speak above the clamor: "And I? May I say nothing, my lord?" In response, Justice Wills, with a wave of his hand, signaled the guards to remove the prisoners from his sight. They were hustled to cells in the basement and made to wait for the hearselike conveyance that would transport them to prison. Already bankrupted and disgraced, Wilde had been sentenced to hard labor so that he might be broken in body as well.

The sad fate of Oscar Wilde—hated, hounded, and hunted to death—terrified other homosexuals, both of his generation and of several beyond. A contemporary observer was probably not exaggerating when he reported that in the days following the trial, the boats out of Great Britain were crowded with men like Wilde, eager to avoid the punishment that he had suffered. And for many decades after, the mere mention of Wilde's name was enough to frighten many homosexuals into silence.

Wilde's destruction revealed the fragility of the double life that homosexuals in late Victorian England had devised to protect themselves. The closet where men like Wilde kept their homosexuality hidden from general view could come down like a house of cards; the thin partition that protected homosexuals from prosecution and persecution was no match for the long arm of the law.

And yet, what survives of Wilde's writing are works of drama and fiction that imagine a world where the vulnerability to exposure that always haunts such double lives has become a thing of the past. Sometimes, this is a matter of perfecting the methods of secrecy. In *The Picture of Dorian Gray*, the protagonist is granted a magic method to avoid apprehension for his secret passions. Other times, the fear that one's secret desires will be exposed is even more radically transcended. In *The Importance of Being Earnest*, Wilde summons the vision of a world where such desires need not be secret in the first place, because they have been cooperating with the law of respectability all along.

What Wilde could not have known, but would perhaps have appreciated, is how the legend of his life and martyrdom have been enlisted as a rallying point for a century-old struggle to put a very different end from the one he imagined in his fiction and his plays to the secrecy that made people like him always vulnerable to attack. Wilde's very name is inseparable from several generations of struggle for homosexual consciousness and

Aesthetic movement

Similar to the Decadence movement in France, the Aesthetic movement took place in the late Victorian period from around 1868–1901, and is considered to have ended with the trial of Oscar Wilde. The rally cry for the Aesthetic circle was France's Théophile Gautier's famous proclamation, "Art for Art's Sake." The Aesthetes, deeply influenced by Oscar Wilde's teacher at Oxford, Walter Pater, believed the arts should provide refined sensuous pleasure, rather than convey moral messages, contradicting the popular Victorian belief that art should be something moral or useful. Instead, the Aesthetes believed art need only be beautiful. Sensuality, symbols, and correspondence between words, colors, and music were important aspects. Writers and artists associated with the movement included Swinburne, James McNeill Whistler, Dante Gabriel Rossetti, and Oscar Wilde, who became the most popular spokesman for the movement.

liberation. The story of Wilde's persecution gave unprecedented publicity to the love that had previously seldom dared to speak its name. "No doubt," noted Havelock Ellis, a celebrated scientist of sexuality, "the celebrity of Oscar Wilde and the universal publicity given to the facts of the case by the newspapers may have brought conviction of their perversion to many inverts [homosexuals] who were only vaguely conscious of their abnormality, and, paradoxical though it may seem, have imparted greater courage to others." If, as Ellis goes on to remark, the Wilde case "can scarcely have sufficed to increase the number of inverts," it certainly increased the number who were conscious of the desires that defined them as such in the eyes of society.

And, "paradoxical though it may seem," the Wilde case, and countless others like it, have imparted greater courage to men and women who have for more than a century ceaselessly labored to bring about a day when gays and lesbians can live free from the fear that they will meet the same disaster. The picture of Oscar Wilde has haunted the minds of many homosexuals who have sought to liberate themselves and others like them from shame and terror. Whatever success these struggles against an intolerant society have enjoyed over the past century owes something to the memory of a man who paid so dearly for his own defiance of it.

two

A Fantastic Figure

A most intense young man
A soulful-eyed young man:
An ultra-poetical super-aesthetical
out of the way young man.

—*Patience,* Gilbert & Sullivan

OSCAR FINGAL O'FLAHERTIE WILLS WILDE was born on October 16, 1854, in Dublin, Ireland, the second son of William Wilde, a scientist and writer, and Jane Elgee Wilde, an Irish nationalist and poet. In a city famous for its talk, Sir William Wilde was known as the best conversationalist in town; in a country where dramatic defiances of England's long-standing rule were common, Lady Wilde was a distinguished figure. "The long pending war with England has actually commenced," she declared in 1848, and she wrote throughout her life in favor of Irish rebellion. "I should like to rage through life," Lady Wilde wrote in December of 1848, "this orthodox creeping is too tame for me, this wild rebellious, ambitious nature of mine." During his tour of the United States in the early 1880s, Wilde would hear his mother, who called herself Speranza, hailed as "one of Ireland's noblest daughters ... who ... in the troublous times of 1848 by the works of her pen and her noble example did much to keep the fire of patriotism burning." (Lacey) If Wilde learned from his father the pleasures of the arresting anecdote and well-turned phrase, his mother taught him the delights of the insurrectionary statement and the dramatic gesture.

Lady Wilde was no less dedicated to the liberation of women than to the liberation of Ireland: "We have now traced the history of women from Paradise to the nineteenth century," she announced in "The Bondage of Woman," an essay, "and have heard nothing ... but the clank of fetters." An essayist, translator, folklorist, and one of the most prominent Irish poets of the 19th century, Lady Wilde, like her famous son, was also known for her talent for making scenes. During the trial of the editor of the *Nation* for seditious (i.e. advocating rebellion against England) publications, including poems that she had written, she stood up in the courtroom and exclaimed, "I, and I alone, am the culprit, if culprit there be."

Her contempt for conventional jewelry and morality made the towering (nearly six feet tall) Lady Wilde a remarkable figure in Dublin, festooned in huge, often inexplicable outfits and exotic headgear. To one St. Patrick's Day ball she wore a dress made of "three skirts of white silk ruched round with white ribbon and hooped up with bouquets of gold flowers and green shamrocks." The dull tones of "respectability" were unendurable to her: "You must never employ that description in this house. It is only tradespeople who are respectable. We are above respectability." Part cartoon character, part voice of conscience; part Irish revolutionary and feminist, part aristocrat and snob, Lady Wilde passed on all she was to her son.

In addition to the two children that he had with Lady Wilde, Sir William had three more, the offspring of premarital relationships. While they were never officially recognized as such, Sir William cared for these three as his own. The terms of this double life were well established for the Victorian gentleman: official and respectable family on one side, illegitimate attachments on the other. Wilde may have learned from his father's example: the partition that divided the father's existence would divide the son's as well. Until his trial brought the show to a close, Wilde, like the heroes, victims, and villains of his fiction, sought always to play at least two roles at once: on one hand, Wilde was a father and husband, on the other, he was the lover of young men; on one hand he was an artist, a phrasemaker, and a friend of the high and mighty, on the other hand, he was a homosexual, pursuing his desires in secret. But while Wilde may have learned from his father the lesson of the double life, he eventually declined to maintain the societally mandated distance between public and private lives.

In school, Wilde met his first love, the one by which all those that followed would be judged. The object of Wilde's schoolboy passion was not a living person, though, but rather a body of

classical literature. Greek and Latin formed part of the core curriculum of schools like Portora, in the Irish town of
Enniskillen, where the upper classes of the British empire
received their education. Knowledge of these languages was
imparted as a sign of high culture, one that separated the elite
from everyone else. To know Greek and Latin was to wear the
badge of a class thought fit to rule those classes that did not
know them. But the study of Greek and Latin was driven more
deeply into Wilde than the marks of status are generally
thought to go. In the philosophy and literature of Greece and
Rome, Wilde deciphered a distant realm of strange passions
and noble aspirations that was no less real to him than the
streets of Dublin and London, the salons of high society, or the
cells of Reading Gaol. To this realm Wilde would always return
whenever he was called upon to explain or defend his life.

While his classmates at Portora, where he was sent in February 1864, knew that Wilde was an excellent and dedicated
student of the classics, what they remembered better was his
reputation as a storyteller, a reputation that began as soon as he
could talk. Before the dazzling dinner table repartee and salon
soliloquies that would put him on the top of London society's
A list, Wilde's golden tongue was already amusing, astonishing,
or provoking family, friends, and classmates. In his telling and
retelling, the events of everyday life quickly became fabulous
adventures; annoyed neighbors or parents became murderous
giants; minor feats of skill were metamorphosed into Homeric
deeds of courage and genius.

Factual accuracy was no match for the thrill of the story,
once Wilde got hold of it; the pleasure that he gave through his
tales, and the pleasure he took from them, had nothing to do
with their correspondence to the truth. "Romantic imagination
was strong in him," one friend noticed, "but there was always
something in his telling of ... tale[s] to suggest that he felt his

hearers were not really being taken in." The fascinating liar, endowed with "a natural gift for exaggeration," whom Wilde celebrates in the essay "The Decay of Lying" is no doubt modeled on himself. "People have a careless way of talking about a 'born liar,' just as they talk about a born poet. But in both cases they are wrong. Lying and poetry are arts—arts, as Plato saw, not unconnected with each other.... As one knows the poet by his fine music, so one can recognize the liar by his rich rhythmic utterance."

Wilde left Portora in 1871 victoriously, one of three pupils to win a Royal School scholarship to study at Trinity College in Dublin. His name was inscribed on a board at Portora reserved for students who won such distinction. Twenty-five years later, after the trials that destroyed his reputation, Wilde's name was erased from the board by school authorities, ashamed that so infamous a character had graduated from their school. His name has since been restored.

At Trinity, Wilde's tutor was the Reverend J.P. Mahaffy, a prominent scholar of ancient history, whom Wilde would later call "my first and best teacher," the man who "showed me how to love Greek things." If Wilde deepened his love for old things at Trinity, he also clothed himself in contemporary trends, adopting in particular the doctrines and costumes of a new cultural sensation known by its friends and enemies as Aestheticism. The Aestheticism that Wilde encountered in his youth emerged from Pre-Raphaelitism, a mid-Victorian school of art and poetry whose work is marked by luxurious medieval settings and hyperbolic metaphors of erotic intensity. Like any fashion movement, Aestheticism had its signature styles: androgynous clothes, long hair, languid attitudes, and a lush devotion to "the beautiful" in all its manifestations, especially the human body in passion or repose.

"If you're anxious for to shine in the high aesthetic line as a man of culture rare," instructs the poet in the comic opera *Patience*, in which Gilbert and Sullivan anatomize the affectations of the Aesthetes,

> You must lie upon the daisies and discourse in novel phrases of your complicated state of mind,
> The meaning doesn't matter if it's only ideal chatter of a transcendental kind ...
> Though the Philistines may jostle, you will rank as an apostle in the high aesthetic band,
> If you walk down Piccadilly with a poppy or a lily in your medieval hand.

"At length their long kiss severed, with sweet smart," Algernon Swinburne declares in the first line of "Nuptial Sleep," a sonnet that contains many of Aestheticism's motifs and mannerisms:

> At length their long kiss severed, with sweet smart:
> And as the last slow sudden drops are shed
> From sparkling eaves when all the storm has fled,
> So singly flagged the pulses of each heart.
> Their bosom sundered, with the opening start
> Of married flowers to either side outspread
> From the knit stem; yet still their mouth, burnt red,
> Fawned on each other where they lay apart.
>
> Sleep sank them lower than the tide of dreams,
> And their dreams watched them sink, and slid away.
> Slowly their souls swam up again, through gleams
> Of watered light and dull drowned waifs of day;
> Till from some wonder of new woods and streams
> He woke, and wondered more: for there she lay.

Not surprisingly, Aestheticism had its critics. In "The Fleshly School of Poetry," Robert Buchanan attacked its "whirl of aesthetic terminology" in terms that resemble contemporary condemnations of sexually explicit art. About "Nuptial Sleep," Buchanan writes: "Here is a full-grown man, presumably intelligent and cultivated, putting on record for other full-grown men to read, the most secret mysteries of sexual connection, and that with so sickening a desire to reproduce the sensual mood, so careful a choice of epithet to convey mere animal sensations, that we merely shudder at the shameless nakedness." Buchanan's essay is a catalog of what many people felt were Aestheticism's crimes: according to the judgment Buchanan delivers, Aestheticism is not only pornographic, it is also pretentious, morbid, and annoying: "these fantastic figures of the fleshly school, with their droll mediaeval garments, their funny archaic speech, and the fatal marks of literary consumption in every pale and delicate visage."

This "pale and delicate visage" hints at another aspect of Aestheticism at least as bothersome to its critics as any other. The outlandish affectations and explicit eroticism of this cult of Beauty amounted to an offense against an anxiously defended norm of masculinity. Enemies of aestheticism such as Buchanan were outraged by the specter of effeminacy that they saw clinging to the "fantastic figures" of this new cult of beauty, with its admiration for exquisite decorations of art or nature. Buchanan gave voice to what many felt when he accused the Aesthetes of promoting a kind of "hermaphrodit[ism]."

As his career progressed, Wilde would figure more and more prominently in the fortunes of Aestheticism, eventually becoming a kind of poster child for the movement, as well as its chief philosopher. But, even in college, he was a confirmed member of the cult; already at Trinity he was winning friends and enemies for his outrageous clothes and opinions.

Among Wilde's friends at Trinity, there were some he would meet again. Wilde would have special reason to remember Edward Carson, a classmate who had come with him from Portora, a serious, studious boy, less brilliant but no less ambitious than Wilde himself. He would have reason to remember that the sober boy was a close friend, at least when they first arrived at Trinity, until Wilde's "flippant approach to life" became too much for Carson. Wilde would have reason to remember that he and Carson had strolled about campus with their arms wrapped around each other, in the style of 19th-century schoolboys. But they grew apart at Trinity and lost touch altogether after that. The next time they met, it was across a courtroom: Carson grew up to become the star Inquisitor in the First Act of the protracted courtroom drama

Punch

Founded by Henry Mayhew and a wood engraver named Ebenezer Landells, *Punch*, a British magazine of humor and satire, ran from 1841 until it closed in 2002. In 160 years, the magazine, which was responsible for the modern use of the word "cartoon," published more than 500,000 cartoons. Over the years, *Punch* developed an international reputation for its witty, irreverent cartoons, which documented and satirized both politics and social life. In the Victorian age, *Punch* was milder, and less inclined to attack the establishment. However, the cartoons of this period present a memorable picture of Victorian England's social life. In particular, the illustrator George Du Maurier created a dandy, flamboyant figure to represent Oscar Wilde, and inevitably helped to make Wilde the public emblem of the Aesthetic movement before Wilde had even published a book. The caricatures of Wilde and the Aesthetic circle were enormously popular with the public.

that Wilde called, with uncharacteristic absence of understatement, the trial for his life.

But long before that fateful encounter came an event in Wilde's life that was no less momentous for him: after his second year at Trinity, Wilde left Ireland to study at Magdalen College at Oxford. "[T]he two great turning points of my life were when my father sent me to Oxford, and when society sent me to prison," he would later write in *De Profundis*. At Oxford, Wilde was an arrogant and often brilliant student, especially in classics, philosophy, and modern literature.

Wilde was also determined to remake himself at Oxford into an upper-class Englishman, abandoning or suppressing any mark of Irishness that he could. The Ireland that Wilde knew as home was hardly impoverished: his parents were at the center of the nation's cultural elite. Nevertheless, Ireland was still a colonial province in the eyes of the members of the English upper classes with whom Wilde sought acceptance. If an Oxford education meant learning new things, it also meant forgetting old ones: "My Irish accent," Wilde once remarked, "was one of the many things I forgot at Oxford." And in its place were the sterling silver intonations that would characterize Wilde's speech for as long as he lived, an aristocratic English that bore no trace of his homeland. Wilde's linguistic assimilation was part of a broader effort to identify with the English, as Richard Ellmann, his foremost biographer, remarks: "In a poem 'Ave Imperatrix,' he would speak of 'our English land,' as though he had been born east of the Irish Sea." There were aspects of his Irishness that Wilde could not lose though, aspects that haunted his life and work in ways that his biographers and critics are only now beginning to assess.

But if Wilde sought entry into the English elite, as represented by Cambridge and Oxford, he certainly did not plan to get there by dressing like everyone else. He made a policy of formal wear at all times. "If I were all alone marooned on a desert island ... I should dress for dinner every evening," he declared to one friend. But Wilde's sartorial flair extended beyond dressing for dinner: the colors of his ties and the shapes of his hats made him a standout even among the other fashion plates at Oxford. Just as it would do later in life, Wilde's striking figure—his lavish garb dressed a six-foot three-inch frame—got him into trouble, although here his enemies were not the press, or the police, but rather fellow classmates annoyed by his aesthetic affects and affectations. One tale from his Oxford days has Wilde, dressed to the nines, dragged by a group of jocks to the top of a hill, where he got up, dusted himself off, and remarked, "the view from this hill is really very charming." Persuaded to try out for the crew team, Wilde would row only at his own, languid pace, despite the voluble exhortations of teammates. There was only one "outdoor game" he was good at, he later remarked: "I am afraid I play no outdoor games at all. Except dominoes. I have sometimes played dominoes outside French cafés."

For all his preciousness, Wilde was, in the words of one Oxford friend, "far from being a flabby aesthete." The muscularity of his aestheticism was demonstrated one night when a group of students decided to beat him up. Instead of the wimp they expected to trounce, they encountered a formidable fighter—one strong enough to beat all of them. Afterward, Wilde led the many spectators who had gathered to watch back to the rooms of one of the assailants, where he invited everyone to help themselves to drinks.

Wilde's own rooms were always well decorated, full of lilies, expensive furniture, and fine china. The rigors of luxury, a favorite subject of his ironic wit, inspired his first recorded epigram: "I find it harder and harder every day to live up to my blue china." It was a *bon mot* heard around the world, or at least around England. Not for the last time, Wilde's studied flippancy alarmed the clergy. An Anglican priest at Oxford condemned it at length: "When a young man says not in polished banter, but in sober earnestness, that he finds it difficult to live up to the level of his blue china, there has crept into these cloistered shades a form of heathenism which it is our bounden duty to fight against and to crush out."

Wilde's Blue China Statement is a Pledge of Allegiance to the details of interior decoration, an allegiance that was to last until the day he died. "The wallpaper and I are engaged in mortal combat," Wilde is claimed to have declared from his deathbed. For all its apparent silliness, though, Wilde's proclaimed commitment to things like blue china, the right flower arrangements, and the best chefs was, in the words of the subtitle he attached to *The Importance of Being Earnest*, a Trivial Comedy for Serious People. Wilde's rhetorical commitment to the frivolous was a weapon in a lifelong war against self-styled Seriousness and Piety. The trivial pose and studied self-indulgence that scandalized his enemies were part of Wilde's arsenal against the hypocritical self-righteousness of the State, Society, and the Church, a self-righteousness that concealed its intolerance under the banner of moral purity.

During Wilde's time, the intellectual atmosphere of Oxford was dominated by two professors, John Ruskin and Walter Pater, who represented the two most prominent schools of thought about art in the second half of the 19th century. For Ruskin, the value of art is measured by its service to an external morality. Art, according to Ruskin, is good or bad depending on the moral values it espouses. For Pater, on the other hand, the value of art dwells entirely in its own effects. Art, according to Pater, has nothing to do with external standards of morality; it can only be judged by standards specific to art alone. Pater thus extended a long line of thought about art and beauty often associated with the philosopher Immanuel Kant, a tradition that emphasizes the difference between art and the world outside of it. Pater radicalized this removal of art from life: according to his lights, art is for art's sake alone; beauty is a sufficient aspiration in itself. The pursuit of the beautiful in art has no other responsibilities: it is not to be determined or deterred by canons of realism or morality.

Pater's teaching and his writing were taken as guides by the Aesthetes, who found in his *Studies in the History of the Renaissance* their most suggestive and persuasive defense. In a phrase that would reappear in *The Picture of Dorian Gray*, Wilde referred to the "strange influence" that Pater's book had over his life. Just as the "low musical cadences" of a certain "yellow book" hold Dorian Gray under their spell, *The Renaissance* never ceased to exert an influence over Wilde's work.

In the famous conclusion to the book, Pater identifies a heightened sense of beauty borne from a sense of life's transience:

> We have an interval, and then our place knows us no more. Some spend this interval in listlessness, some in high passions, the wisest, at least among "the children of this world," in art and song. For our one chance lies in expanding that interval, in getting as many pulsations as possible into the given time. Great passions may give us this quickened sense of life, ecstasy and sorrow of love, the various forms of enthusiastic activity ... which come naturally to many of us. Only be sure it is passion—that it does yield you this fruit of a quickened, multiplied consciousness. Of such wisdom, the poetic passion, the desire of beauty, the love of art for its own sake, has most. For art comes to you proposing frankly to give nothing but the highest quality to your moments as they pass, and simply for those moments' sake.

These words made many people nervous in the late 19th century as they do today. Abolishing rules of evaluation by which different forms of "passionate attitudes" could be embraced as wholesome, or rejected as sinful, Pater appears to accept all of them. What was, and is, inspiring or ominous about this passage is that it appears to aid or abet any "desire of beauty," including those that the State might prosecute, and Society scorn. If art was for art's sake alone, if art was its own justification, so was the "ecstasy and sorrow of love" concentrated in art, ecstasies and sorrows that could hardly be confined to the limits allowed by the family novel or G-rated movie.

Though Wilde found Ruskin edifying and reassuring—"the dearest memories of my Oxford days are my walks and talks with you," he wrote him—it was Pater who won his heart. Even so, he later turned against his mentor. Pater could never go far enough for Wilde: he discovered the shadows of erotic desire in art, but in a lifeless academic style that could never touch its substance; he intimated the attitudes of passion to be found in a painting or a poem, but never the passions themselves. "Was he ever alive?" Wilde asked when he was told that Pater had died. Still, the rejected teacher made a lasting mark on the bolder student; glimpses of Pater's personality show up all over Wilde's work; his unfinished study of art was the beginning of Wilde's own. It remained for Wilde himself to find in the vague attitudes that Pater traced a more vivid sexuality; it remained for Wilde to make erotic desire an explicit subject of art and thus to enter a danger zone that the cautious professor always feared to tread.

At Oxford, Wilde was drawn as well to the intellectual and spiritual intensities of the Roman Catholic Church. Such an interest alarmed Wilde's Protestant family, especially his father, perhaps in part because of the hints of dissident sexual passion woven into the extravagances of Catholic dress and ceremony.

What made Wilde's family nervous about his attraction to the Catholic Church resembles what made many families nervous about Pater's effects on their young sons: the specter of corrupting influences, a specter never far removed from the possibility of homosexuality. The rumors of homosexuality attached to the church were especially lively in the wake of John Henry Newman's conversion in the middle of the century. Newman, a charismatic and persuasive religious leader, was at the center of the Oxford Movement, which sought to restore more mystery and ritual to the Anglican church. For many of its detractors, such devotion was little more than a chance for men to wear dresses and admire the muscular bodies of saints and martyrs in pain and rapture, all in the exclusive company of other men.

Wilde loved what he called the "perfume of belief" and all its rich decor. He was attracted to what attracts Dorian Gray during his own brief fling with Catholicism:

> to kneel down on the cold marble pavement, and watch the priest, in his stiff flowered vestment, slowly and with white hands moving aside the veil of the tabernacle, or raising aloft the jewelled lantern-shaped monstrance with that pallid wafer.... The fuming censers, that the grave boys, in their lace and scarlet, tossed into the air like great gilt flowers, had their subtle fascination for him.

As this passage might suggest, Wilde's flirtation with Catholicism, whatever else it may have been, was a fashion statement and an aesthetic experience, one of those "high passions" that Pater recommended to his readers. Still, the effects of this flirtation were long lasting. Well after the pictures of the pope and the bust of the Madonna were removed from his rooms, Wilde would return again and again to the central concepts and icons of the church, not as literal doctrines of belief, but as analogies and metaphors to illuminate the world of his fiction.

There are very few early accounts of the young Wilde in love. His first expressions of romantic and erotic attraction are letters and poems, such as this sonnet, inspired by a portrait of a young man:

> A fair slim boy not made for this world's pain,
> with hair of gold thick clustering around his ears ...
> Pale cheeks whereon no kiss hath left its stain
> Red under-lip drawn in for fear of Love,
> and white throat whiter than the breast of dove—

This poem anticipates one of the central impulses of Wilde's work: the urge to sequester the beauty of youth from the damages of time and passion. But there were other worldly damages from which Wilde sought protection as well. The poem was written in 1877 but revised by Wilde four years later to convert the boy into a girl. The uneasiness reflected in this sex change suggests the prevailing atmosphere of anxiety about homosexuality, which was especially intense at Oxford and Cambridge in the second half of the 19th century. Even the slightest glimpse of it resulted in eruptions whose tremors were felt campuswide. All it took was Walter Pater to sign "yours lovingly" in a letter to a homosexual student named William Money Hardinge for scandal to result.

When Benjamin Jowett, the master of Balliol, the house at Oxford where Hardinge resided, was informed of Hardinge's "crimes," he initiated an investigation against him. Jowett was disturbed by the specter of homosexuality despite, or perhaps because of, his own investment in something that looked a lot like it. A distinguished classicist, Jowett was an influential scholar and advocate of the forms of devotion between men described by Plato. But he was made nervous by a cult of Hellenism that emerged in the 19th century, a Hellenism that celebrated versions of such devotion between men that hovered near the sexual. Many classical scholars of the 19th century solved this problem by simply excising anything overtly homosexual from the text. In *Maurice* (1914), E.M. Forster's novel about the trials of homosexual self-discovery, this tradition of timidity, called bowdlerizing, is condemned as scholarly dishonesty:

> They attended the Dean's translation class, and when [the class] was forging quietly ahead Mr Cornwallis observed in a flat toneless voice: "Omit: a reference to the unspeakable vice of the Greeks." Durham observed afterwards that he ought to lose his fellowship for such hypocrisy ... "I regard it as a point of pure scholarship. The Greeks, or most of them, were that way inclined, and to omit it is to omit the mainstay of Athenian society."

Jowett's own solution was not to censor those elements of Plato that might be interpreted as encouraging sexual relations between men, but rather to translate them into terms compatible with a modern aversion to homosexuality: according to his account, the love between men that Plato describes is a nonsexual devotion; it is, in the commonplace sense of the term, platonic. Another, somewhat more strained strategy enlisted by Jowett to avoid the appearance of homosexuality was to transform the object of passion that Plato describes from a man into a woman. "Had he lived in our own times he would have made the transposition himself," Jowett argued. As Wilde's revision of his own poem suggests, this ruse was hardly confined to the classical scholar. Neither was it confined to the 19th century: a strategic shift in the gender of a lover or a friend has been a favored means of concealment for generations of gay men and lesbians. Gay men and lesbians have long found it a convenience, and sometimes a real lifesaver, to know that as easily as "Victor" becomes "Vicky," the appearance of homosexuality can be avoided.

The punishment of men like William Money Hardinge (he was suspended, or "sent down," as a consequence of the charges against him) for taking their Plato too literally suggests the incendiary potential of the classics in the Victorian period. Like the early Protestants who found in their own reading of the Bible a faith that set them at odds with the established guardians of the Holy Scriptures, students of the classics like Hardinge and Wilde discovered a new meaning in the old texts, a meaning denied or obscured by generations of interpretation or misinterpretation, a meaning no less revolutionary than the one that abetted the Protestant Reformation. Out of the stories the Greeks and Romans told of passionate devotions between soldiers, shepherds, and philosophers, men like Wilde fashioned a heroic mirror for their own suppressed desires, a mirror that afforded even ordinary men, such as Forster's Maurice, the shock of recognition: "I have always been like the Greeks and didn't know."

Men like Jowett were placed in an awkward position when it came to dealing with men like Hardinge and Wilde, an awkwardness that reflected the conflicting attitudes of their culture, and perhaps our own, about devotion between men. The difference between the kind of love between men that Jowett found to celebrate in Plato, and the kind of love between men that Jowett found necessary to condemn is the difference between something at the center of his culture and something that seemed to threaten it. Jowett's influence extended far beyond the precincts of classical scholarship: as

master of Balliol College, Jowett instructed and inspired generations of the British upper classes, young men who would go
on to staff the higher echelons of England and its empire.
Devotion to others like oneself is an indispensable ingredient
for such work. As the army knows, a man has to love the men
he serves with to be a good soldier. But, as the army also knows,
he cannot love them too much if he is to satisfy the requirements of a culture as homophobic as Wilde's, or our own.
While Jowett enthusiastically approved of the forms of male
bonding that bred loyalty to one's country, one's class, and
one's race, the kind of male bonding that made (and makes)
men cohere into athletic teams, combat units, and political
factions, such bonding had to be rigorously separated from
anything that appeared to be sexual. Men like Hardinge, and
later of course Wilde himself, were punished for confusing
socially acceptable, indeed, socially induced, forms of male
bonding with socially unacceptable ones.

In the summer of 1876, between his junior and senior years
at Oxford, Wilde toured Greece and Rome. The excursion was
momentous: Wilde came face to face with the remainders and
reminders of the intellectual and spiritual traditions that had
incited and inspired him. In a place in Greece called Katakolo,
with his old teacher J.P. Mahaffy, Wilde witnessed some of the
excavations that were then taking place of Olympia, and he later
claimed that he had been on hand when the statue of Apollo was
removed from the ground. "Yes, during the excavation I was present when the great Apollo was raised from the swollen river. I
saw his white outstretched arm appear above the waters. The
spirit of the god still dwelt within the marble." This story, like so
many others, is cast in doubt by Wilde's biographers. But
whether he saw what he says he saw at Katakolo, Wilde's vision
of the spirit of a god in a statue's "white outstretched arm" fore-
sees a figure that will raise itself repeatedly to the surface of his

texts: the statue or the painting that merges with the spirit or the flesh of the beautiful body it is made to represent.

If Greece was the home of classicism, Wilde's next destination was the capital of Catholicism. Two years earlier, Wilde had to cancel a tour of Rome for lack of funds; now he was finally to see the Holy City and meet the pope. His private audience with Plus IX moved Wilde beyond words—for a few minutes anyway, before he wrote a poem about the experience, later published. David Hunter Blair, a friend who had converted to Catholicism and dearly hoped that Wilde would too, was convinced that his mission was finally done.

But Wilde had too many Gods to serve to settle on just one. In addition to the Anglican church, with all the backing of his father and other friends, there were also the glories of Hellenism he had just witnessed in Greece. No less than his encounter with the pope, Wilde was affected by his pilgrimage to the grave of Keats, a poet whose "effeminacy, languor and voluptuousness" were, for Wilde, "the characteristics of that 'passionate humanity' which is the background for true poetry." In one letter, Wilde confessed that Keats's grave, although merely "a hillock of green grass with a plain headstone," was to him "the holiest place in Rome."

When asked later about his religion, Wilde remarked, "I don't think I have any. I am an Irish Protestant." Whatever Wilde's articles of faith were, they certainly were not to be confined by any official church, especially not any that sought to deny or restrain the alarming passions that Wilde had discovered with delight in art and literature. Back at Oxford, Wilde raised a stir in the Magdalen chapel when he was to read the weekly lesson from the Bible on "The Three Appointed Feasts." To the assembled congregation, which included Queen Victoria's youngest son, Wilde chose to recite a different biblical text instead:

The Song of songs, which is Solomon's.
Let him kiss me with the kisses of his mouth:
for thy love is better than wine ...

"You have the wrong lesson Mr. Wilde," the dean shouted. "It is Deuteronomy 16." But for Oscar Wilde, it was the right one after all.

three

The Critic as Artist

To live well, in Wilde's view, was to turn oneself into an artifact—to savour each of one's moments with the unique intensity of a poem. Art was thus not a substitute for living, but the very model for it. In his dress, speech, deportment, in the minutiae of his daily conduct, Wilde [strove] to live with the elegance and self-completion of a great painting or a symphony—to allow each of his varied inclinations free realization, and to shape them in provisional harmony. Such supreme freedom of self-expression was for him the very essence of morality

—Terry Eagleton

WILDE FINISHED OXFORD IN A BLAZE of glory all the more intense for being unexpected. A brilliant but irreverent student, he triumphed in his final examinations, much to the surprise of school authorities: "The dons are 'astonished' beyond words— the Bad Boy doing so well in the end!" But the Bad Boy didn't know what to do next. He applied halfheartedly for a position as school master; his mother wanted him to enter politics. With his prospects unclear, and with a little money he had inherited from his father, who had died in 1876, Wilde moved to London in 1878.

There his colorful costumes, good-natured exhibitionism, and theatrical affectations made him, if not, as he boasted, "the most prominent figure in society," at least famous enough to be the subject of dinner table conversations, magazine cartoons, and popular operas. His knack for the witty comeback quickly became the talk of the town. "There goes that bloody fool Oscar Wilde," someone remarked within his earshot: "It's extraordinary," Wilde declared with delight, "how soon one gets known in London!" At a dinner in the Haymarket Theatre, after taking as much of Wilde's wit as he could, W.S. Gilbert, of Gilbert and Sullivan, turned to him and remarked: "I wish I could talk like you. I'd keep my mouth shut and claim it as a virtue." "Oh that would be selfish," Wilde remarked in response. "I could deny myself the pleasure of talking, but not to others the pleasure of listening."

Wilde's talent for the last word is built into a rhetorical form that became his trademark: the epigram. What iambic pentameter, the heroic couplet, or the paragraph are for some writers, the epigram was for Wilde: the basic building block of his literary achievements. If one sets out to find an example of an epigram, "a pointed or antithetical saying" according to the Oxford English Dictionary, chances are one will land on one by Wilde, the universally acknowledged lord of the genre. Raymond Chandler, an American writer of detective stories in the 1930s and 1940s, once remarked that while he filled his stories with plot twists because his readers demanded them, his real concern was for the details of the Los Angeles landscapes where the stories took place. His investment shows: the plots of his whodunits are forgotten as soon as they are read, but the streets and flowers of Southern California take up permanent residence in the memory. What is true of the Los Angeles landscape in the work of Raymond Chandler is true of the epigram in the work of Oscar Wilde. Indeed, his letters, plays, reviews, and stories sometimes seem to be little other than a storehouse for epigrams: even after everything else about them is forgotten, the epigrams that ornament his writing, like jewels in a rusted crown, remain vivid to the mind.

When Wilde remarks in "Phrases and Philosophies for the Use of the Young" that "To love oneself is the beginning of a life-long romance," or when Algernon declares in *The Importance of Being Earnest* that "all women become like their mothers. That is their tragedy. No man does. That's his," no reply is appropriate, or even imaginable. In the epigram, Wilde's legendary proclivity for the last word has its lasting monument.

During his years in London, Wilde befriended James McNeill Whistler, the American artist famous for his Impressionist landscapes and cruel humor. Wilde was full of admiration for the artist, who in turn was full of admiration for himself. Throughout their often acrimonious relationship, Whistler was obsessed with the suspicion that Wilde stole ideas from him, as their most famous exchange indicates. Although there are many variants of the story, the punchline is the same: Whistler says something witty; Wilde says, "How I wish I had said that." Whistler replies: "Don't worry, Oscar, you will."

Indeed, Wilde's writings and sayings are a quilt of quotations borrowed from others, frequently himself. Oxford refused Wilde's gift of his first book of poems on the grounds that they were nothing but a tissue of allusions to other poets. He thought nothing of transferring his own epigrams from text to text. For Wilde, such quotation was not a matter of plagiarism; rather it reflected a recognition that the ways that the artist, or anyone else, sees things is arranged by the culture and society that she or he inhabits. Originality for Wilde was not a matter of making something out of nothing, but rather of the creative enlistment of what is already made. "It is only the unimaginative," he remarked in 1885, "who ever invents. The true artist is known by the use he makes of what he annexes, and he annexes everything."

In London, Wilde wrote his first play, *Vera; or, The Nihilists*, and distributed copies to actresses he knew, hoping that they would want the lead role for themselves. The play revolves around a band of revolutionaries who plot the assassination of the Russian czar. *Vera* was more than timely—Revolutionary and Reactionary activity in Russia were often in the news—it was too timely: the assassination of Czar Alexander II made it impossible to open the play.

In 1881, Wilde published a controversial collection of poems, filled with classical allusions and Aesthetic sentiments: *Punch* called it "Swinburne and water;" other reviews accused it of insincerity and indecency. It did win praise from significant sources, though: Matthew Arnold, the spokesman of Victorian High Culture, liked it; so did John Addington Symonds, an early and cautious apologist for homosexual rights.

Among the poems in this volume is "Charmides," the story of a sailor who falls in love with a statue of Athena. The poem recalls the vision of the god that Wilde saw surface at Katakolo, and it anticipates the story of a beautiful boy who exchanges fates with a painting in *The Picture of Dorian Gray.*

> A little space he let his greedy eyes
> Rest on the burnished image, till mere sight
> Half swooned for surfeit of such luxuries,
> And then his lips in hungering delight
> Fed on her lips, and round the towered neck
> He flung his arms, nor cared at all his passion's will to check.

"Charmides" is one of Wilde's earliest mergings of aesthetics and erotics—of the work of art and the object of sexual desire. This marriage of art and sexuality is a departure from a traditional emphasis on art's *disinterestedness*: theories of aesthetics usually describe the passion for art as a kind of refined love that needs nothing from the thing it adores. What makes the love of art different from the hunger for food or the desire for sex, according to this tradition of thought, is that the art lover does not need art: his devotion is disinterested. Moreover, the love of art is traditionally reputed to be metaphysical—it transcends the desire of and for the flesh. Thus, when Wilde has Charmides "fe[e]d on [Athena's] lips in hungering delight," the love of art merges with the kind of passion from which it is traditionally separated.

Richard D'Oyly Carte, theatrical producer for Gilbert and Sullivan, invited Wilde in 1881 to tour America in conjunction with the opening there of *Patience*, a parody of Aestheticism whose protagonists were modeled on Wilde himself. D'Oyly Carte enlisted Wilde as a living specimen of "an aesthetical man," a walking, talking display that would give Americans a chance to see the original that Gilbert and Sullivan were lampooning. Already a celebrity whose every move was covered by the press, Wilde during his American excursion was the subject of wide editorial commentary, both at home and in the States. One friendly journalist wrote of Wilde, "the Americans are far more curious than we are to gaze at those whose names, for one reason or another, have become household words. And in this I think they are wiser than we are, for it is difficult to realize the personality of anyone without having seen him. Mr. Wilde, say what one may of him, has distinct individuality and, therefore, I suspect that his lectures will attract many who will listen and look."

Remarks like this demonstrate what was already a crucial aspect of Wilde even early in his career: by the early 1880s, he was more than a man, a poet, or a playwright—he was a celebrity. The American tour changed Wilde's life; it solidified his celebrity status and made him over into a mass-market product. "Oscar Wilde Forget-Me-Not Waltzes," musical scores featuring Wilde, cartoons, replicas of his trademark sunflower: the form varied, but the commodity was always Oscar Wilde.

Wilde's commodification may best be seen as part of a broader cultural development—the rise of advertising as the means of fame. At the historical moment that modern advertising was emerging as the main means of publicity in our culture, Wilde was busy advertising himself. What has become a commonplace notion for us—the sense that famous people are essentially brand names, like Pepsi or Nike—was comparatively new a hundred years ago, and its invention is significantly associated with Wilde's own exertions. When Wilde, arriving in the United States, remarked to the customs officer at New York harbor, "I have nothing to declare but my genius," he was characteristically outrageous and accurate: his principle commodity was his own personality.

The American tour was largely a triumph, earning Wilde new friends and followers. Often the inevitable parodies were funny. One journalist claimed that Wilde was being paid by

P.T. Barnum to accompany jumbo the Elephant, while wearing his trademark lily and sunflower. But aversion to him here, as in England, often could not help but sound as if it were fueled by more than merely "literary" distaste. Edmund Gosse, an English writer who took it upon himself to warn American journalists about Wilde, described his poetry as "a curious toadstool, a malodorous parasitic growth"; Henry James called him "an unclean beast."

On January 18, 1882, a momentous interview took place: an interview between Oscar Wilde, exponent and embodiment of English Aestheticism, and Walt Whitman, the great American Romanticist, at the poet's home in Camden, New Jersey. Already, by the 1880s, the affection for other men that is a central part of Whitman's poetry had helped encourage homosexual writers, both American and English. For men like Wilde and his contemporaries at Oxford, Whitman's unembarrassed affection for men inspired them to express their own.

Wilde saw in Whitman an early exponent of an aesthetic and erotic sensibility "much misunderstood in our own time." After the meeting, Wilde declared: "He is the grandest man I have ever seen, the simplest, most natural and strongest character I have ever met in my life. I regard him as one of those wonderful, large, entire men who might have lived in any age.... Strong, true and perfectly sane, he is the closest approach to the Greek we have yet had in modern times." "The kiss of Walt Whitman is still on my lips," Wilde announced after his encounter with him, and he was not the only one amazed by their meeting. While we may be tempted to read this encounter as a meeting of two prophets of gay liberation, it is important to recall that both men had ambivalent and often ambiguous relations with homosexual people and homosexual topics. One of the consequences of Wilde's conviction is that it obscures the fact that he was never fully part of the small band of activists in late-19th-century England who made explicit defenses of homosexuality their project. He kept himself mostly aloof from frank professions of homosexuality, and from those who made them. Wilde's homoeroticism, like Whitman's, was seldom interested in naming itself as such.

The American tour helped revivify Wilde's sense of ethnic identity. His Anglification initially left Irish Americans cold. The Irish-American press condemned him at first: SPER-ANZA'S SON OSCAR WILDE LECTURES ON WHAT HE CALLS THE ENGLISH RENAISSANCE; PHRASING ABOUT BEAUTY WHILE A HIDEOUS TYRANNY OVERSHADOWS HIS NATIVE LAND. During the course of his tour, Wilde's ethnic pride and his resentment about the English occupation of Ireland became visible. When asked for his response to the killing of England's secretary for Ireland, Lord Cavendish, in Dublin by a group of Irish nationalists, Wilde remarked, "when liberty comes with hands dabbled in blood it is hard to shake hands with her. We forget how much England is to blame. She is reaping the fruit of seven centuries of injustice."

Wilde's politics were contradictory; along with his commitment to social justice came an indefatigable commitment to social climbing. On one hand, he insisted on his devotion to Irish republicanism while on the other he was careful to sustain and expand his connections with the English aristocracy. "Of course," Wilde declared to an American interviewer, "I couldn't talk democratic principles to my friend the Prince of Wales. That you understand is simply a matter of social tact."

In Leadville, Colorado, he was transported by bucket into the Matchless Mine, where he participated in two ceremonies with the miners. First he presided over the opening of a new shaft, called, in his honor, The Oscar: "I had hoped that in their grand simple way that they would have offered me shares in The

Oscar," Wilde remarked, "But in their artless untutored fashion they did not." Dinner followed. "The amazement of the miners when they saw that art and appetite could go hand in hand knew no bounds." The miners cheered when he lit a cigar. When he downed glass after glass of whiskey without effort, they hailed him as "a bully boy with no glass eye." Wilde approved of a sign at the casino in Leadville: "Please Don't Shoot the Pianist. He is doing his best." "I was struck with this recognition of the fact that bad art merits the penalty of death and I felt that in this remote city, where the aesthetic applications of the revolver were clearly established in the case of music, my apostolic task would be much simplified as indeed it was."

After returning from New York to London, Wilde left almost immediately for Paris in 1883, where he exchanged his Aesthetic fashions for a new, somewhat more somber style, more in keeping with the traditional understated elegance of the gentlemen of the day. He cut his long hair and tossed out his sunflowers in favor of more restrained dress. *Punch* magazine made fun of the change with this mock advertisement:

> To be sold the whole of the stock in trade, Appliances and Inventions of a Successful Aesthete who is retiring from business. This will include a large Stock of faded Lilies, dilapidated sunflowers and shabby Peacock's Feathers, several long haired wigs, a collection of incomprehensible poems and a number of impossible pictures. Also an invaluable manuscript work entitled "Instructions to Aesthetes" containing a list of Aesthetic catchwords, drawings of Aesthetic attitudes and many choice secrets of the craft. Also, a number of well dressed dadoes, sad coloured draperies, blue and white china and brass fenders.... No reasonable offer refused.

But if Wilde tossed out his outrageous Aesthetic costumes, it was only to make room in his closet for an even more shocking fashion. While in Paris, Wilde became acquainted with the work of the *Decadents*, a literary movement centered around writers such as Charles Baudelaire, Paul Valéry, and Paul Verlaine devoted to the dark side of sexual and artistic passions. For its enemies, such as Max Nordau, the author of the influential reactionary tract *Degeneration*, the decadents were symptoms and agents of a widespread cultural decline associated with the end of the century.

For Wilde, the most important Decadent document was Joris-Karl Huysmans's *À Rebours* (Against nature), which had been published in 1884. Huysmans's novel catalogs the outlandish pleasures of Des Esseintes, a super-refined dandy who hates all things natural. In *The Picture of Dorian Gray*, Wilde describes a "yellow book," which resembles the style and substance of Huysmans's work in particular and calls to mind the Decadents more generally:

> There were in it metaphors as monstrous as orchids, and as subtle in colour. The life of the senses was described in the terms of mystical philosophy. One hardly knew at times whether one was reading the spiritual ecstasies of some medieval saint or the morbid confessions of a modern sinner. It was a poisonous book. The heavy odour of incense seemed to cling about its pages and to trouble the brain. The mere cadence of the sentences, the subtle monotony of their music, so full as it was of complex refrains and movements elaborately repeated, produced ... a form of reverie, a malady of dreaming.

The French Decadents expanded the vocabulary of Wilde's aesthetic and erotic imagination. More exactly, they expanded his vocabulary for imagining these things together, to make art a kind of sexual experience, and sexual experience a kind of art. The strains of the Decadents reverberate throughout Wilde's work; they are especially loud in "The Sphinx," which he had begun in the early 1870s but did not feel inspired to complete until after his excursion to France 10 years later. In the questions that he puts to the ancient figure of the sphinx, a silent statue that has seen everything and who tells nothing, Wilde projects a universe of exotic passion. Among the images that flash across the screen of "The Sphinx" is Antinoüs, the beautiful boy whom the emperor Hadrian took as his lover:

> You heard from Adrian's gilded barge the laughter
> of Antinous
> And lapped the stream and fed your drouth and watched
> with hot and hungry stare
> The ivory body of that rare young slave with his
> pomegranate mouth!

Such hints of homosexual desire fed rumors about Wilde's sexuality, rumors which had became more and more pointed by the early 1880s. His effeminate manners and exotic interests prompted *Punch* to call him a "Maryanne," a term for a homosexual, and *The New York Times* to describe him as "epicene." Coincidentally or not, Wilde about this time began to seek a wife in earnest. In 1883, he began courting Constance Lloyd, whom he married in May 1884.

Mr. and Mrs. Wilde took up residence in the West End of London, at 16 Tite Street, where they promptly began to live beyond their means. "It is only by not paying one's bills that one can hope to live in the memory of the commercial classes," Wilde declared, and he did all he could to make himself indelible to them. The Wildes' house and their social lives were lavish. So were their clothes. Wilde boasted to one friend that their costumes had attracted a crowd: "A number of rude little boys surrounded and followed us. One boy, after staring at us, said, ''Amlet and Ophelia out for a walk, I suppose!' I answered, 'My little fellow, you are quite right. We are!'"

Oscar and Constance Wilde were frequently asked to dinner, often by the same people who would not have associated with the outlandish bachelor. Wilde made fun of his new respectability, just as he made fun of everything else about himself. When he asked the novelist Olive Schreiner why she lived in the East End, she answered, "Because the people there don't wear masks." "And I live in the West End," Wilde remarked, "because the people there do." Completing the family picture were two sons, Cyril, born in 1885, and Vyvyan in 1886.

A husband and then a father with little fortune to fall back on, Wilde needed to make money. During the 1880s, he wrote

Labouchere Amendment

From the 16th century to the early 1800s, sodomy—defined as any kind of non-reproductive sexual act—was punishable by death in Britain. Executions ended in 1836, and sodomy was removed from the list of capital crimes in 1861. However, sodomy was still considered a crime, and in 1885, Parliament adopted the Criminal Law Amendment Act. The passage of the act included Section 11, also known as the Labouchere Amendment, which widened the definition of illegal homosexual acts to include "gross indecency," making all sexual activity between men illegal. The crime was punishable with up to two years in prison, with or without hard labor. The law, dubbed the "blackmailer's charter," cast a shadow of criminality over British gay men until its repeal 82 years later.

hundreds of reviews for the *Pall Mall Gazette, Nineteenth Century, Dramatic Review*, and the *Woman's World*, a journal that he also edited. Erudite and opinionated, the style of Wilde's reviews parodies the critic's authority; they are a campy combination of omniscience and officiousness. His judgments are often one sentence executions: "though not passionate he can play very prettily with the words of passion, and his emotions are quite healthy and quite harmless." On Swinburne's later work, Wilde expresses his disappointment: "His song is nearly always too loud for his subject.... It has been said of him, and with truth, that he is a master of language, but with still greater truth it may be said that language is his master."

Beyond his occasional reviews, Wilde wrote a series of essays on aesthetics that have had a lasting impact on the way that art and literature are read. Essays like "The Decay of Lying" (1889) and "The Critic as Artist" (1890) have helped shape our own conception of the relation between fiction and reality. In his trademark tone of bratty didacticism, Wilde reasserts in these essays the familiar Aesthetic insistence on art's separation from the world. Art is not a reflection or representation of the world, it "never expresses anything but itself"; art offers no practical benefit: "all art is quite useless."

The critic's task, Wilde declares in "The Critic as Artist," is no more to represent art than the artist's task is to represent nature. He thus refutes Matthew Arnold's canonical declaration on the critic's duty:

> It has been said by one whose gracious memory we all revere ... that the proper aim of Criticism is to see the object as in itself it really is. But this is a very serious error, and takes no cognizance of Criticism's most perfect form, which is in its essence purely subjective.... For the highest Criticism deals with art not as expression but as impression.

The critic's duty is less a matter of vision than revision; less the work of description than imagination. Just as Wilde declares the artist free from the constraints of external reality and thus encouraged to consult his own imagination, he insists that the critic's first duty is to his own impressions.

But Wilde does more than merely declare again art's independence from the real world; he insists upon its superiority: "My own experience is that the more we study Art, the less we care for Nature. What Art really reveals to us is Nature's lack of design, her curious crudities, her extraordinary monotony, her absolutely unfinished condition." Art is not merely autonomous from nature and reality; it actually shapes it: "Paradox though it may seem—and paradoxes are always dangerous things—it is none the less true that Life imitates art far more than Art imitates life.... A great artist invents a type, and Life tries to copy it."

> What is nature? Nature is no great other who has borne us. She is our creation. It is in our brain that she quickens to life. Things are because we see them, and what we see, and how we see it, depends on the Arts that have influenced us.... People see fogs, not because there are fogs, but because poets and painters have taught them the mysterious loveliness of such effects. There may have been fogs for centuries in London. I dare say there were. But no one saw them, and so we do not know anything about them. They did not exist till Art had invented them.

Wilde's proposition that Art helps create the Reality that it is supposed merely to reflect figures prominently in one of the central movements of modern thought. A wide range of philosophers, scientists, psychologists, and artists have shown that what we think of as objective reality is partly produced by the very forms of representation that are enlisted to describe objective reality. Thus, for example, in *The Structure of Scientific Revolutions*, the philosopher Thomas Kuhn has demonstrated that the paradigms scientists use to chronicle the natural world actually shape rather than merely reflect it.

If Wilde's allegiance to artifice works to support the general sensibility of modernity, it works as well, if more quietly, to disable one of the most familiar arguments against dissident sexualities. Rejecting the simple separation of "the natural" from the "unnatural," Wilde implicitly rejects the crude system of evaluation which identifies the first category with virtue and the second with vice. If the category of "the natural" is itself a product of culture, if "the natural" and "the artificial" are confused with one another rather than opposed to one another, then it makes no sense to congratulate one kind of sexuality for its "naturalness" or condemn a different kind for its "unnaturalness."

In *The Importance of Being Earnest*, someone is supposed to be attending "a more than usually lengthy lecture by the University Extension Scheme on the Influence of a permanent income on Thought." Although no one in the play seems to care about such things, Wilde himself had much to say about the effects that economics exert on the mind. Indeed, he actually wrote a version of the lecture that no one hears in *The Importance of Being Earnest* several years before, in the form of an essay called "The Soul of Man Under Socialism."

Wilde was intensely, if sporadically, interested in the struggles for social justice that the hedonistic dandy that he produced for the stage, and played in his own life, could only disdain. Like Lord Goring, a "flawless dandy" in *An Ideal Husband* who finds time between smoking cigarettes and contemplating the perfection of his buttonholes to have a hand in saving England, Wilde made room in his hectic social schedule to attend meetings of the Fabian Society, a socialist organization led by activist intellectuals such as George Bernard Shaw and Beatrice and Sidney Webb. When Shaw passed around a petition in support of the labor activists implicated in the 1886 Chicago Haymarket Riots, Wilde was at first the only person willing to sign. "We are all more or less Socialists now-a-days," Wilde declared in 1894. "1 think I am rather more than a Socialist. I am something of an Anarchist, I believe, but, of course, the dynamite policy is very absurd, indeed."

The essay advocates a *bon vivant* brand of communism, a socialist utopia of freedom and luxury for all. "[B]y converting private property into public wealth, and substituting cooperation for competition," and thus "ensur[ing] the material well-being of each member of the community," Wilde argues that Socialism, contrary to its reputation as agent of a drab conformity, will furnish the conditions necessary for individuality to flourish:

> The chief advantage that would result from the establishment of Socialism is, undoubtedly, the fact that Socialism would relieve us from the sordid necessity of living for others, which, in the present condition of things, presses so hard upon almost everybody.... The majority of people spoil their lives by an unhealthy and exaggerated altruism—are forced, indeed, so to spoil them. They find themselves surrounded by hideous poverty, by hideous ugliness, by hideous starvation. It is inevitable that they should be strongly moved by all this.

The institution of private property ruins what Wilde calls Individualism first by creating a class of have-nots whose legitimate clamor distracts others from the task of self-development. It also subverts Individualism by presenting a phony version of it that eclipses the real thing:

> Private property has really harmed Individualism, and obscured it, by confusing a man with what he possesses. It has led Individualism entirely astray. It has made gain, not growth, its aim. So that man thought that the important thing was to have, and did not know that the important thing is to be. The true perfection of man lies, not in what a man has, but in what man is. Private property has crushed true Individualism, and set up an Individualism that is false. It has debarred one part of the community from being individual by starving them. It has debarred the other part of the community from being individual by putting them on the wrong road, and encumbering them.

"The Soul of Man Under Socialism" is not the only place where Wilde takes the measure of capitalism's effects. In his poems, plays, and stories, Wilde describes a world where the commodity form rules, a world where monetary value eclipses everything else. The omnipotence of money appears everywhere on the surface of Wilde's texts as an explicit theme. In *The Importance of Being Earnest*, Lady Bracknell declares the same girl she had earlier dismissed to be "a really attractive young lady" once she discovers her to be worth "A hundred and thirty thousand pounds! And in the Funds!" She speaks for many others in Wilde's work, for whom money is a central motive.

But the power of money that Wilde measures extends beyond the greed of certain comic or sinister characters; it influences the atmosphere of his work in subtler ways as well. In *The Philosophy of Money* (1900), the sociologist Georg Simmel describes the marketplaces of capitalism as so many "nurseries of cynicism." The cynic's conviction that any sense of "difference in values" is an

> illusion ... can be most effectively supported by money's capacity to reduce the highest as well as the lowest values equally to one value form and thereby to place them on the same level, regardless of their diverse kinds and amounts.... The more money becomes the sole centre of interest, the more one discovers that honour and conviction, talent and virtue, beauty and salvation of the soul are exchanged against money ... the more a mocking and frivolous attitude will develop in relation to these higher values that are for sale for the same kind of value as groceries, and that also command a "market price."

The cynicism that Simmel describes is the prevailing climate in Wilde's fiction and plays. "I was in hopes he would have married Lady Kelso," one bored character remarks in *A Woman of No Importance*, "But I believe he said her family was too large. Or was it her feet? I forget which." Wilde tells different versions of this joke again and again; the punchline is always the same: there is finally no difference between things that seem incomparable. This joke reflects a culture of capitalism, where distinctions in quality are leveled by the commodification of everything.

By the end of the 1880s, Wilde's reputation as a writer was secure. In addition to his essays, he published *The Happy Prince and Other Tales* in 1888, a collection of fairy tales, as well as a variety of other stories and poems. What lay ahead were the novel and the plays that would win Wilde the reputation that he has today; what lay ahead were the works that would make him one of the most loved and hated English writers of the last hundred years.

four

Portrait of the Artist as a Gay Man

You, Mr. Gray, you yourself, with your rose-red youth and your rose-white boyhood, you have had passions that have made you afraid, thoughts that filled you with terror, day-dreams and sleeping dreams whose mere memory might stain your cheek with shame.

—from *The Picture of Dorian Gray*

IF, AS SOME OF HIS BIOGRAPHERS suggest, Wilde was moti-
vated to marry in part to put an end to the rumors of his
homosexuality, it would not be surprising: the last decades of
the 19th century were thick with anxiety about the "love that
dare not speak its name." Such anxiety was hardly anything
new in England: the distinguished jurist William Blackstone
spoke for a long tradition when, in Commentaries on the Laws
of England (1769), he characterized sodomy as "the infamous
crime against nature." But the condemnation of "peccatum
illud horribile inter christonos non nominandum" took on new
force in England during the later part of the 19th century.
While "sodomy" had been a crime in England since 1533, until
the middle of the Victorian period the term was only vaguely
defined. Sodomy referred to a whole range of sexual activities
linked only by the fact that they were not defined by the goal of
procreation. The historian Jeffrey Weeks describes how this
amorphousness persisted late into the 19th century:

> The phrase with which Sir Robert Peel forbore to mention
> sodomy in Parliament, "the crime inter christonos non nom-
> inandum" ... was widely used to cover all forms of
> non-procreative sex well into the nineteenth century. In
> 1854 Sir George Rickards, a political economist, used the
> same phrase in fulminating against birth control, and as late
> as 1868 the parliamentary candidature of Lord Amberley
> (Bertrand Russell's father) was marked by press attacks on
> him for advocating "unnatural crimes" (meaning contracep-
> tion). "Sodomy" was a portmanteau term for any forms of
> sex that did not have conception as their aim, from homo-
> sexual acts to birth control.

But in the late 19th century, the law against homosexuality,
male homosexuality in particular, became more specific. On

one hand, executions for "buggery"—anal intercourse between men—ceased in 1836, and it was taken off the list of capital crimes in 1861. On the other hand, while the law had been severe on the subject of "buggery," it had been silent about various other kinds of homosexual practice. In 1885, Section 11 of the Criminal Law Amendment Act was passed by Parliament. Section 11, known for its author as the Labouchere Amendment, defines a new crime: "acts of gross indecency," which made all sexual activity between men illegal:

> Any male person who, in public or private, commits, or is a party to the commission of, or procures or attempts to procure the commission by any male person of any act of gross indecency with another male person, shall be guilty of a misdemeanor, and being convicted thereof shall be liable at the discretion of the court to be imprisoned for any term not exceeding two years, with or without hard labour.

The Labouchere Amendment worked to criminalize all forms of homosexuality; it also worked to sharpen its distinct character, to draw it out from the vague and general category of deviant sexuality where it had been previously located, and give it pride of place: while *sodomy* had included a broad range of activities, *gross indecency* referred to and highlighted male homosexuality.

This change in English law needs to be cast in the light of a couple of general developments that occurred over the course of the last half of the 19th century. It was during this time that the modern study of sexuality was born. Pioneers in the field like Richard von Krafft-Ebing and Havelock Ellis cataloged the range of sexual practices and proclivities and characterized these practices and proclivities as the way of defining individuals. Their studies worked to replace a religious model for judging sexuality with a "scientific" one. The blunt and often violent prosecution of "sodomy" inspired by a simple religious sense of sinfulness gave way as the century progressed to a more refined, and in some ways a more effective, criminalization and pathologization of the now specific crimes of homosexuality. Less severe, but more pervasive, this new regime of sexual regulation helped to establish a new degree of awareness and of apprehensiveness about homosexuality, both among those who practiced it and those who did not.

The expansion of the legal campaign against male homosexuality that took place in England during the last part of the 19th century, and which culminated in the Labouchere Amendment, was due in part to a greater awareness of homosexuality, per se. This campaign against homosexuality was also fueled by a cult of masculinity and chastity propagated by religious leaders, educators, and politicians of the Victorian period. The pressure we feel today to be sexually "normal" and the threat of dire consequences for self, family, or nation if we fail to live up to this norm are partly the effect of this 19th-century craze for sexual (rather than political) correctness. Jeffrey Weeks paraphrases the terror that inspired this fad:

> Let one crack appear in the moral order and floods of lustfulness would sweep society away. In their minds the syndromes of schoolboy masturbation, public-school "immorality" (meaning homosexuality) and prostitution were closely intertwined. The progress of civilization, the Rev. J.M. Wilson, Headmaster of Clifton College, Bristol, intoned, was in the direction of purity. This was threatened by "sins of the flesh," which threatened self and nation. He advised his students to "strengthen your will by practice; subdue your flesh by hard work and hard living;

by temperance; by avoiding all luxury and effeminacy, and all temptation."

The apocalyptic anxiety Weeks reports here, the sense that sexual deviation threatens to destroy the individual who practices it and the nation that tolerates it, made those who practiced homosexuality not mere sinners but enemies of the State.

So homosexuality was not merely something for Victorian sexologists to study with academic calmness; it was a flash point for deep-seated and widespread fears about the integrity of masculinity; it was a threat to be watched for and discouraged by the combined forces of science, the law, and the guardians, both secular and religious, of public morality. The fear of homosexuality was fueled as well by sensational scandals circulated in the popular press. In the second half of the 19th century, sex in general, and male homosexuality in particular, became a staple mass-media story in England. Scandals like the Boulton-Park case in 1870, involving two transvestites who solicited sex with men, and the Cleveland Street affair 20 years later, involving a ring of male prostitutes with an aristocratic clientele, helped to make homosexuality something frightening and fascinating for the Victorian imagination.

If this climate of homophobia inclined Wilde to marry in the first place, it was not enough to keep him content playing the part. Out shopping one day with his wife, Wilde came across a group of good-looking young men: "something clutched my heart like ice." The coldness that clutched Wilde's heart was the fearful recognition that is the first stage of the process we call coming out; it is the freezing fear that arises when, in a homophobic culture, a repressed desire for one of our own gender suddenly surfaces and makes itself known to us.

By the middle of the 1880s, life as father and husband had

become a bore for Wilde, the marriage contract too much like a prison sentence. He loitered more and more in the company of attractive young men and quickly ensconced himself at the center of a circle of young male admirers, charmed by his literary prestige and eloquence, his refined defiance of social convention, and his radiant wit. He first encountered Robert Ross, a young Canadian preparing to take the entrance exams for King's College at Cambridge, in 1886, when the boy was 17; by 1888, they were lovers. By all accounts, this was the older man's first homosexual encounter, and, by all accounts, it was Ross who pursued Wilde. Ross was boyish, witty, and easygoing, and the two got along well. They developed a lifelong friendship that outlasted their brief love affair: Ross remained loyal to Wilde until the end.

In the late 1880s, Wilde's circle included a group of young poets, writers, and artists: André Raffalovich, Richard Le Gallienne, Bernard Berenson, and John Gray, whose good looks inspired Wilde to name the hero of his novel after him. The specter of the Cleveland Street affair, which broke open in 1889, was vivid for the homosexual culture that Wilde inhabited; the disgrace of Lord Arthur Somerset, who had been forced by the scandal to flee England, was a clear warning to people like Wilde and his friends that while membership in the ruling class of British society may have had its privileges, those did not include blanket immunity from police prosecution. However elegant their dinner parties, however powerful their family connections, however prestigious or promising their own reputations, members of the upper class were nonetheless vulnerable to the wrath and fear of a society and a legal system that regarded homosexuality as an abomination. The passion that drew Wilde and his friends together was compelled to remain the love that dare not speak its name, at least not very openly. "You know, you and I," Wilde wrote to

André Raffalovich, "we must be most careful of the people we are seen with."

Thus Wilde and his friends lived a high-society version of the life-style that contemporary gay culture calls the closet. According to the terms of this double life, private passion was guarded by public reticence and caution. Wilde avidly pursued attractive men, both in person and in his letters. "I want so much to see you: when can that be?" he wrote to Richard Le Gallienne: "Friendship and love like ours need not meetings, but they are delightful. I hope the laurels are not too thick across your brow for the to kiss your eyelids." "The world is

Cleveland Street Affair

In 1889, one year before the publication of Oscar Wilde's *Picture of Dorian Gray*, a sensational scandal involving homosexuality, aristocracy, and government cover-up erupted in London. The story, which first broke in the North London Press, reported that the aristocrats Earl of Euston and Lord Arthur Somerset were regular customers at a male brothel, and hinted that Prince Eddy, son of the Prince of Wales, was also involved. The reporter claimed the British government had protected these prominent figures. In response to the story, Lord Somerset safely fled the country, but the Earl of Euston remained in England and sued the reporter for libel. Although the reporter was sentenced to twelve months in prison for refusing to reveal his sources, when the criminal trial began, the government conspiracy theory re-emerged. Parliament member Henry Labouchere, who drafted the Gross Indecency Law, moved to form a committee to investigate the government; however, the cover-up was never exposed. Although the story gradually faded from the headlines, the sensational scandal had lasting affects on public views toward homosexuality, and helped set the vindictive mood for the trials of Oscar Wilde six years later.

changed because you are made of ivory and gold," Wilde declared to John Gray, "The curves of your lips rewrite history." But if such passion moved the earth that Wilde walked upon, it was compelled, nonetheless to remain hidden from most of the world.

In order to conduct their affairs undetected, homosexuals in Victorian England, like homosexuals elsewhere, before and after, devised sometimes elaborate codes to communicate with one another. Wilde himself had a hand in developing such codes for the culture he inhabited, esoteric emblems that only the initiated would understand. The most famous of these was the green carnation, which Wilde imported from France and made the trademark of his circle. Combining, as he was fond of doing, his exhibitionism and his love of exclusivity, Wilde, at the opening of his play *Lady Windermere's Fan*, arranged for several of the actors and members of the audience "in the know" to wear this secret sign of homosexuality. The flower became notorious. "[A]ll the men who wore them looked the same," Robert Hichens declares in a parodic novel about the Wilde circle called *The Green Carnation*. "They had the same walk, or rather waggle, the same coyly conscious expression, the same wavy motion of the head. When they spoke to each other, they called each other by Christian names. Is it a badge of some club or some society, and is Mr. Amarinth [Wilde] their high priest? They all spoke to him, and seemed to revolve round him like satellites around the sun."

At the same time that Wilde was immersing himself in the upper-class homosexual culture of late Victorian England, his writing began to approach homosexual subjects. In 1889, he published "The Portrait of Mr. W.H.," a story about young men taken with a theory that Shakespeare's love sonnets are addressed to a beautiful boy named Willie Hughes, a portrait of whom the author of the theory has in his possession. While the details of this theory were original to Wilde's story, the general sense that the sonnets were homoerotic was not. It was widely assumed by Victorians that at least one of the people to whom Shakespeare addressed his love poems was a man. Like the subject of ancient Greek literature and history, Shakespeare's sonnets were full of homosexual resonances in late-19th-century England. Benjamin Jowett summarized a general nervousness about the sonnets when he declared that fondness for them was "neither manly or natural. It shows a sympathy with Hellenism."

In Wilde's story, the portrait of Mr. W.H., like everything else associated with the theory that Willie Hughes is the beloved person addressed in Shakespeare's sonnets, proves a forgery. Nevertheless, despite all the evidence that discredits it, the narrator of the story remains sympathetic: "[S]ometimes, when I look at it, I think that there is really a great deal to be said for the Willie Hughes theory of Shakespeare's Sonnets."

The narrator's tenacious belief that love poems written in the 16th century preserve a beautiful boy from the ravages of time defies the rules of evidence. By the end of the story, there is simply no reason to believe it. But the narrator's conviction conforms to one of Wilde's own dearest articles of faith, the one borne by the spirit of Apollo that he claimed to witness in a statue dredged from the sea; the article of faith unveiled at the Greek temple where Charmides' desire for a goddess transforms a statue into passionate flesh. Under the magic wand of Wilde's imagination, the work of art is resurrected as an adorable and animate body; conversely, the adorable and animate body is endowed with the permanence of art. Wilde admits not the requirements of reason, but his own deepest hope when at the end of "The Portrait of Mr. W.H.," he affirms that "Willie Hughes's true tomb" is less a crypt for a corpse than it is a work of art where the beautiful young body lives forever in the sonnets he inspired:

> Willie Hughes's true tomb ... was the poet's verse, his true monument the permanence of the drama. So it had been with others whose beauty had given a new creative impulse to their age. The ivory body of the yellow Bithynian slave rots in the green ooze of the Nile, and on the yellow hills of the Cerameicus is strewn the dust of the young Athenian; but Antinous lived in sculpture, and Charmides in philosophy.

In "The Portrait of Mr. W.H.," artistic ambition converges with homosexual passion. The beautiful body, rescued by the hand of artist or philosopher from the decay of time and certain death, is here not just *any* body: it is the body of a man loved by other men. It may well be the composite figure of the scores of beautiful young men who provoked Wilde's deepest desires; it may well remember the boy at Oxford whose left thigh Wilde had called a "sonnet"; the beautiful young poet whose eyelids Wilde longed to kiss; the face, shimmering with admiration, virility, and receptiveness of the young men who crowded around the finest wit of the age.

Wilde had once before depicted the body preserved by its removal to the house of art as an adorable male form: "The Portrait of Mr. W.H." restores the original gender of the adored body in the sonnet inspired by a painting that Wilde had written while still an undergraduate (see chapter two). Willie Hughes restores to view the male form that Wilde erased when he revised that poem for publication. But "The Portrait of Mr. W.H." crowns this form with the laurel leaves reserved for William Shakespeare. The adored male form is here preserved not by just any painter or poet, such as the artist, now forgotten, who made the portrait that inspired Wilde's equally forgettable poem, but by the premier poet and playwright of English literature.

With this story, Wilde's flouting of social convention approached the danger zone of late Victorian culture, the zone where sensibilities are outraged enough by some act of defiance against the rigors of heterosexism that they set out to retaliate. Reviewers grumbled and insinuated, but they mostly held their fire for a work by Wilde that went further still.

The basic plot of what was to become *The Picture of Dorian Gray* had been on Wilde's mind for a long time: a beautiful young man trades places with his portrait; the portrait suffers all the damages of age, while the young man remains forever young. Wilde's tale was an answer to a forlorn prayer that he had been heard to murmur a few years before he wrote the story, while looking at a portrait of himself. "What a tragic thing it is. This portrait will never grow older, and I shall. If it was only the other way." For years Wilde had been telling the story of a young man who gets what he himself wished for, but it had always been a private entertainment, a fantasy he shared with a select audience composed mostly of boys and young men who often looked a lot like Dorian Gray himself.

Wilde's decision to go public with *The Picture of Dorian Gray* was made one night in 1889, at a dinner hosted by the American publisher of a new journal called *Lippincott's Monthly Magazine*. Another literary luminary of the period was present as well. Arthur Conan Doyle, best known as the literary creator of Sherlock Holmes, later called Wilde a madman, but he was impressed enough with him that night to record the details of their conversation years later. It was not the first time that Wilde's capacity to amuse managed to charm even those who were uneasy about him, nor would it be the last. Late in the evening, after Wilde had entertained the guests with his parables and stories, the conversation turned to contributions for the journal. Doyle suggested that the editor might publish a Sherlock Holmes story he had just written called "The Sign of Four." As soon as Doyle had finished telling his story, Wilde began to describe his idea for *The Picture of Dorian Gray.* By the time the evening was through, the editor had arranged to publish both stories. Thus a night of pleasant conversation and casual competition was the beginning of what was to become one of the great cultural fire storms of the 19th century.

It is no doubt true, as some critics have recently suggested, that Wilde's trial and conviction for acts of gross indecency with other men five years after the publication of *The Picture of Dorian Gray* make the story difficult to read as anything other than a tale of homosexuality; it is no doubt true, as critics have recently suggested, that Wilde's text is actually somewhat more ambiguous than this reading would admit. Nevertheless what we now recognize as homosexual desire is certainly a central theme of the novel: "The lad certainly was beautiful," his mentor muses, and resolves to "make that wonderful spirit his own." Dorian Gray is attractive enough to draw to the surface the erotic dimension that may always lie buried in the relation between a teacher and a student:

> To project one's soul into some gracious form, and let it tarry there for a moment; to hear one's own intellectual views echoed back to one with all the added music of passion and youth; to convey one's temperament into another as though it were a subtle fluid or a strange perfume: there was a real joy in that.

The artist who paints Dorian's picture also confesses his love:

> Dorian, from the moment I met you, your personality had

the most extraordinary influence over me. I was dominated, soul, brain, and power by you ... I worshipped you. I grew jealous of every one to whom you spoke. I wanted to have you all to myself. I was only happy while I was with you.... Weeks and weeks went on, and I grew more and more absorbed in you.

While the subject of homosexuality may be excavated in Wilde's other work, it appears much nearer the surface of *The Picture of Dorian Gray*. The novel's protagonist and the men who surround him are covered in the codes of homosexuality through which Wilde and men like him communicated with one another. Dorian Gray is constantly likened to homosexuals of other times, such as Antinoüs, the emperor Hadrian's lover, or to various other famous and infamous homosexuals from history. Dorian Gray's portrait allows the original to lead a double life, such as the one that Wilde and his friends knew. Dorian Gray bears on his face none of the tell-tale signs of debauchery; the painting bears them for him, thus enabling him to appear as the walking picture of innocence among respectable people. The split lives that both Dorian Gray and Oscar Wilde led are more than coincidentally connected: the dark half of Dorian Gray's double life is lit with a thousand clues of the love that dare not speak its name.

No wonder, then, that Wilde's novel created a sensation. Never before in England had homosexuality been so closely approached in a work of such wide circulation. The press set off alarm bells: a reviewer in the *Daily Chronicle* called it "a tale spawned from the leprous literature of the French *Decadents*—a poisonous book, the atmosphere of which is heavy with the mephitic odours of moral and spiritual putrefaction." "Mr. Oscar Wilde has again been writing stuff that were better unwritten," the *Scots Observer* declared, and while "The Picture of Dorian Gray" ... is ingenious, interesting, full of cleverness, and plainly the work of a man of letters ... [t]he story—which deals with matters only fitted for the Criminal Investigation Department of a hearing *in camera*—is discreditable alike to author and editor. Mr Wilde has brains, and art, and style; but if he can write for none but outlawed noblemen and perverted telegraph-boys, the sooner he takes to tailoring (or some other decent trade) the better for his own reputation and the public morals.

The insinuation could not have been clearer. No one could doubt that among the "matters" in the novel "only fitted for the Criminal Investigation Department" were violations of the Labouchere Amendment, such as those committed by the "outlawed noblemen and perverted telegraph-boys" who were the customers and male prostitutes exposed in the Cleveland Street scandal, still fresh on the minds of the Victorian public.

The Picture of Dorian Gray takes up again the theme expounded in "The Portrait of Mr. W.H." It is again the story of the body of a man that other men desire, changed into a work of art and thus saved from the damages of fleshly existence. This time though, the desired male body, and the men who desire it, are set in the present, rather than a distant past. They do not dwell in a faraway century, but rather among us and within us in the modern world. No longer vivid but remote figures set at a safe distance on the stage of Shakespeare's England or the Olympian reaches of Hellenism, the characters filled with homosexual desire in *The Picture of Dorian Gray* are recognizable contemporaries, people like our neighbors, our brothers, our friends, or ourselves.

Wilde could be speaking for himself when he has the artist in his novel confess what is finally the fatal error of dressing the male model he adores in modern clothing:

I had drawn you as Paris in dainty armour, and as Adonis with huntsman's cloak and polished boar-spear. Crowned with heavy lotus-blossoms you had sat on the prow of Adrian's barge, gazing the green turbid Nile.... And it had all been what art should be, unconscious, ideal, and remote. One day, a fatal day, I sometimes think, I determined to paint a wonderful portrait of you as you actually are.... Whether it was the Realism of the method, or the mere wonder of your personality, thus directly presented to me without mist or veil, I cannot tell. But I know that as I worked at it, every flake and film of colour seemed to me to reveal my secret.

It may not be surprising that when Wilde, immersed in the upper-class homosexual subculture of Victorian England, returned to his favorite figure of the body preserved in art, he should cast that body as male. But Wilde did do something startling when he made that body, and the men who love it, his contemporaries. Inviting inevitable comparisons between himself and the characters that he created, Wilde courted the danger of blowing the door off his own closet. In his pursuit of opportunities to express with ever more vividness the passion for the body sheltered by the house of art, Wilde risked exposing himself by exposing the kind of body for which he himself felt passion. It was a flirtation with candor such as he always liked. "I would go to the stake for a sensation," Wilde boasted, as his affairs with men became easier and easier for the world to surmise. This time, though, Wilde paid dearly for his flirtation. *The Picture of Dorian Gray* would supply ammunition to his persecutors and prosecutors and thus help bring on the disaster that cost Wilde all but his life.

By conforming to what the artist Basil Hallward calls the "method" of "realism" and giving his story a contemporary setting, Wilde removed the shield that protected art from the condemnation of moral censors. According to the aesthetic doctrine that Wilde promoted, the work of art immunized the adored body not only from the ravages of time, but also from the judgments of those who would otherwise castigate such a body as prurient. Art, Wilde had always maintained, was by its nature exempt from moral evaluation. "The sphere of art and the sphere of ethics are absolutely distinct and separate," Wilde declared in a letter to the editor of the *St. James's Gazette*, protesting its condemnation of his novel. "It is to the confusion between the two that we owe the appearance of Mrs Grundy [a fictional character held to epitomize English respectability], that amusing old lady who represents the only original form of humour that the middle classes of this country have been able to produce."

Wilde repeated the claim again and again in defense of *The Picture of Dorian Gray*, first in the novel's preface, then in response to hostile reviews, and finally from the defendant's docket at the trials in which the story was introduced as evidence of its author's homosexuality. This time, though, the argument did not wash: *The Picture of Dorian Gray* was too close to home. Like the work of Robert Mapplethorpe a hundred years later, the controversial gay artist whose photographs were condemned as pornography, Wilde's novel seemed so near real life that in the eyes of many, the exemption from censorship accorded a work of art did not seem to apply.

Having taken up the hints he found in aestheticism, Wilde imagined in *The Picture of Dorian Gray* a sexualization of art beyond Pater's wildest dreams. All the while, though, he continued to rely on the distinction between art and the "real" world to protect him from the condemnation of the intolerant. In the case of his most controversial work, Wilde's effort to have it both ways failed. The novel's "immoral" reputation was to dog him for the rest of his life; it helped the press and the prosecutor's office ruin him; it followed him to his grave. It remained for future generations to imagine a different defense of the kinds of dissident sexual desires and practices for which *The Picture of Dorian Gray* as well as its author were condemned. It remained for future generations to suggest that such desires and practices require, in fact, no defense at all.

chapter
five

Family Comedies

[Wilde] brought comedy back to the London stage. The 19th century was on its deathbed and still he managed to make it laugh at itself.

—Peter Ackroyd

EXIT THE OUTLAW ARTIST, WHOSE expressions of homosexual desire outraged his late Victorian audience and set a time bomb that would explode in Wilde's face several years later; enter the triumphant playwright, whose witty and reassuring domestic dramas won him the laurel of popular acclaim. By the middle of its opening night, two years after the skirmish over *Dorian Gray*, it was clear that *Lady Windermere's Fan* had what it took to capture London. At the end of the evening, bathed in applause from what *The New York Times* called "the most brilliant audience that had gathered for years," Oscar Wilde, with a cigarette in his hand and a green carnation in his button hole, took the stage:

> Ladies and gentlemen: I have enjoyed this evening immensely. The actors have given a charming rendering of a *delightful* play, and your appreciation has been most intelligent. I congratulate you on the great success of your performance, which persuades me that you think almost as highly of the play as I do myself.

It was a performance worthy of Wilde, who in his prose, plays, and everyday life liked nothing so much as the role of impossibly egotistical dandy, ready at the drop of a cigarette ash to claim the lion's share of credit for himself.

The speech and the cigarette annoyed people who did not appreciate that, like everything else about him, these affectations were part of a theatrical role that Wilde almost never stopped playing: "[T]he unspeakable one ... responded to curtain calls by appearing with a metallic blue carnation in his buttonhole and a cigarette in his fingers," his old enemy Henry James sneered; "*Ce monsieur* gives at last on one's nerves." "The artist cannot be degraded into the servant of the public," Wilde defiantly declared a few years later, when asked to defend the self-love of his curtain speeches: "While I have always recognized the cultural appreciation that actors and audience have shown for my work, I have equally recognized that humility is for the hypocrite, modesty for the incompetent. Assertion is at once the duty and privilege of the artist."

Wilde's disdain for social niceties went beyond egotistical pronouncements and bad manners. Throughout the period of his theatrical success (1892–95), Wilde romanced young men with ever more fervor, and ever less anxiety about appearances. During the early 1890s, Wilde hosted lavish dinners and evening parties for good-looking young men of all classes and showered them with gifts and letters. Abandoning his homelife, Wilde took up residence in hotel rooms, where, under the watchful eyes of the staff, he would bring his conquests to spend the night. All of this would eventually catch up with him, but in the meantime, during his days and nights of wine and roses, Wilde pursued his passions with almost no regard for the code of silence and discretion that was the homosexual's only hope of protection in late Victorian England.

We may wonder how it was that Wilde was able to get away with all this. It is a measure of the popularity of his plays that they succeeded despite anything their author said or did, no matter how rude or reckless. All of Wilde's argumentative ingenuity was unable to save *The Picture of Dorian Gray* from the assaults of moral censors; none of his outrageousness was able to subvert the triumph of his plays. The fear and loathing that Wilde provoked with his novel about curious passions was replaced shortly thereafter by the cheers of popular approval that greeted *Lady Windermere's Fan.* Starting with this comic melodrama, and ending only when his disgrace compelled the closing of *The Importance of Being Earnest* and *An Ideal Husband* in 1895, Wilde was the most popular playwright in England. If he was able to get away with unconventional curtain speeches, and even more daring behavior outside the theater, this may be because his plays comforted and delighted his Victorian audience; if Oscar Wilde, the homosexual high roller, was for a while forgiven for his ostentatious dissent from the family values of his time, that may be because Oscar Wilde, the playwright, devoted all of his craft to defending those values.

Wilde's hour of glory on stage did not come easily. His first two plays, set in unfamiliar places and full of bizarre and violent events, were utter failures. *Vera; or, the Nihilists,* when it finally was produced, closed after a brief run and terrible reviews. Wilde could not even get a London opening for *The Duchess of Padua,* which he wrote in 1883; it was not produced at all until 1891, and then only in New York. The critics were scathing: "If this poet was not inspired," *The New York Times* remarked, "he at least tried very hard to be, and certainly thought he was." Late in his life, when he was pressed for money, Wilde was asked to consider publishing the play. "The *Duchess* is unfit for publication," he remarked, "the only one of my works that comes under that category."

All this changed when, with *Lady Windermere's Fan,* Wilde cut out the foreign costumes and exotic backdrops of *Vera* and *The Duchess of Padua* in favor of a story closer to home. In *Lady Windermere's Fan,* Wilde established a plot formula that was his ticket to commercial success. Once he hit upon this formula, the money troubles that had dogged him most of his adult life seemed to be over, once and for all; it was no longer necessary to be constantly borrowing from friends and avoiding creditors. Once he hit upon this formula, Wilde was free at last to really live up to his blue china, not to mention his crystal champagne goblets, his black velvet jackets, and his lavender trousers.

We all know the basic outline of the story that proved so lucrative for Wilde: it has dominated mass entertainment for the past century and a half, from the Victorian novel to the soap opera and the situation comedy. This story is traditionally called the marriage plot, and it has two parts: in the first, a normal, lawful marriage is threatened by infidelity, illegitimacy, or crime; in the second, the threat is contained in one way or another.

The threat to the family that Wilde describes in *Lady Windermere's Fan*, his first domestic drama, is extramarital passion, the desire for someone other than one's allotted spouse. Perhaps after *The Picture of Dorian Gray*, Wilde wanted to reassure his audience that marriage was durable enough to tolerate passions at variance with itself. It may be that after his scandalous portrayal of desires that seemed to reject marriage, Wilde wished to comfort his audience with the thought that wedded love would triumph over the threat posed by other forms of desire.

Lady Windermere is a "proud Puritan," and like all such characters in Wilde's plays, she is educated to understand that the threat of such passions is something that can be managed. As the play begins, her overzealous sense of rectitude has made her susceptible to the blandishments of Lord Darlington, who, wanting Lady Windermere for himself, persuades her that her husband is romantically entangled with Mrs. Erlynne, a dubious woman recently arrived on the social scene. Lady Windermere's predictably severe condemnation of adultery is contrasted with the casual attitude of her friends. The Duchess of Berwick prescribes a foreign vacation as a cure for Lord Windermere's infidelity:

> The whole of London knows it. That is why I felt it was better to come and talk to you and advise you to take Windermere away at once to Hamburg or to Aix, where he'll have something to amuse him. I assure you, my dear, that on several occasions after I was first married, I had to pretend to be very ill, and was obliged to drink the most unpleasant

mineral waters merely to get Berwick out of town, he was so extremely susceptible. Though I am bound to say, he never gave away any large sums of money to anybody. He was far too high principled for that.

For the Duchess of Berwick, a husband's "susceptibility" is a chronic condition that a wife can manage rather than a once-in-a-lifetime catastrophe:

Yes dear, these wicked women get our husbands away from us, but they always come back, slightly damaged, of course. Don't make scenes, men hate them.

According to the Duchess of Berwick, infidelity is more like bad coffee or detergent than a mortal wound. Such affairs depreciate the value of one's marital commodities (now "slightly damaged"); but they can be cured by means of easily purchased mineral waters and foreign distractions; they are hardly lethal.

For Lady Windermere, on the other hand, adultery is simply ruinous. She confronts her husband, who not only denies any impropriety in his relationship with Mrs. Erlynne, but insists that the suspect woman be invited to a party the Windermeres are hosting that evening. Unbeknownst to Lady Windermere, Mrs. Erlynne is actually her own mother, who years before had been persuaded to abandon her husband and daughter by a man who claimed that her husband was unfaithful to her. The eyebrow-raising interviews between Lord Windermere and Mrs. Erlynne were negotiations to buy her silence about her identity. During the ball, Lady Windermere flees to Lord Darlington's chambers. When Mrs. Erlynne comes across the letter Lady Windermere has left behind for her husband, she has a change of heart.

Energized by her newfound maternal love, Mrs. Erlynne

rushes to Lord Darlington's rooms, where she knows she will find Lady Windermere, in order to persuade her to return to her husband. In the midst of their interview, Lord Darlington returns to his chambers, accompanied by a group of friends including Lord Windermere himself. The women hide, but Lady Windermere drops her fan, and her husband sees it: "Speak, sir! Why is my wife's fan here? Answer me! By God! I'll search your rooms, and if my wife's here, I'll ..." Lord Windermere is prevented from searching the rooms by Mrs. Erlynne, who emerges from behind the curtain in order to allow Lady Windermere to escape undetected.

In the scene that follows, Mrs. Erlynne manages to save her daughter from any scandal. She came alone to see Lord Darlington, she claims, having taken Lady Windermere's fan by mistake. In the last act of the play, Lady Windermere promises Mrs. Erlynne that she will keep her own brush with adultery a secret from her husband:

> Lady Windermere: Oh! What am I to say to you? You saved me last night!
>
> Mrs. Erlynne: Hush—don't speak of it.
>
> Lady Windermere: I must speak of it. I can't let you think that I am going to accept this sacrifice. I am not. It is too great. I am going to tell my husband everything. It is my duty.
>
> Mrs. Erlynne: It is not your duty—at least you have duties to others besides him. You say you owe me something?
>
> Lady Windermere: I owe you everything.
>
> Mrs. Erlynne: Then pay your debt by silence. That is the only way in which it can be paid. Don't spoil the one good thing I have done in my life by telling it to any one. Promise me that what passed last night will remain a secret between us. You must not bring misery into your husband's life. Why

spoil his love? You must not spoil it. Love is easily killed. Oh! how easily love is killed. Pledge me your word, Lady Windermere, that you will never tell him. I insist upon it.

And here is the meat of the matter. Here is the most important source of strength for the marriage in its defense against the extramarital passions that menace it. When extramarital passions cannot be trivialized, as they are by the Duchess of Berwick, they must be kept a secret. The rule of secrecy is something that goes back to Wilde's earliest memories of his own home, where his father's premarital shenanigans were an open secret, but a secret nonetheless. It was of course rule number one for people who shared Wilde's own extramarital desires.

After *Lady Windermere's Fan*, Wilde briefly dropped the subject of domestic intrigue and returned to the scenes of exotic passions that had filled his poetry. Written mostly during a visit to Paris in 1891, *Salome* is about the biblical temptress who, failing to seduce John the Baptist, looks for revenge from Herod. Desperate to see her perform the dance of the seven veils, Herod promises to grant her anything she wishes; after the dance, Salome demands the head of the man who rejected her. In the last scene of the play, Herod, revolted by the sight of Salome kissing the severed head of John the Baptist, orders her execution.

Rehearsals were already well under way when the lord chamberlain deemed the play sacrilegious and stopped production. (Censorship of plays did not end in Britain until 1968.) For the lead, Wilde managed to persuade Sarah Bernhardt, whom he later called "The only person in the world who could act Salome ... that 'Serpent of old Nile,' older than the Pyramids." When the examiner of plays denied *Salome* a license, Bernhardt returned to Paris, and Wilde spoke of following her and renouncing his English citizenship. William Archer, a drama critic, exhorted Wilde to stay and fight: "It is surely unworthy of Mr. Wilde's lineage to turn tail and run away from a petty tyranny." Wilde decided against flight from a repressive England. As Ellmann notes, when he made the same decision again two years later, dire consequences followed.

In *Lady Windermere's Fan*, Mrs. Erlynne is so worried about the fragility of married love that she implores her daughter to conceal her extramarital temptation, but in the two domestic dramas that followed, *A Woman of No Importance*, which opened in 1893, and *An Ideal Husband*, which ran in 1895, the love between wives and husbands and between sons and mothers is less easily killed than Mrs. Erlynne makes them out to be. Here, such love is strong enough to endure the

Censorship

The Stage Licensing Act of 1737 significantly impacted the development of theater in Britain. The act was introduced by Prime Minister Robert Walpole, who was concerned that political satire on the stage was undermining him and the authority of the government. The act authorized the government to ban and censor what it considered obscene drama from the public arena. The Lord Chamberlain, a government official, scrutinized and censored each play before it could be performed for the public. Although outright bans were not common, the Chamberlain frequently insisted on changes to a script before giving approval for a performance. For over two hundred years, the Lord Chamberlain's blue pencil marks struck through lines in hundreds of plays, including *Lysistrata* by Aristophanes, George Bernard Shaw's *Mrs. Warren's Profession*, Henrik Ibsen's *Hedda Gabler*, and Oscar Wilde's *Salome*. The government censorship of plays did not officially end in Britain until 1968.

knowledge of sins and crimes that go against it. A woman can go on loving her husband, and a son can go on loving his mother, even though she knows that he has done something awful, like having sex outside of marriage or selling state secrets. In both plays, a secret is confessed and pardoned; in both plays, familial love is generous enough to forgive the sins that seemed able to destroy love.

And in *The Importance of Being Earnest*, Wilde imagines an even bolder reconciliation of familial love and a secret that seems to menace it. For the first time, and the last, Wilde imagines the happy union of familial love and an extramarital passion that seems to threaten it, not by the concealment of the passion, or by a confession of it and repentance for it, but rather by the miraculous discovery that this secret passion, and the marriage that it seems to be opposed to, are really the same thing after all.

The Importance of Being Earnest crowned Wilde's career as a playwright. It opened on Valentine's Day in 1895. The bitter cold of the night did not deter London's High Society from assembling in a scene that one observer described with wide-eyed awe:

> The coachmen in the hansoms breathed upon their numbed fingers for warmth; the horses snorted into the frozen air. Nevertheless broughams, cabs, equipages of all kinds lined both sides of the street, and still they continued to arrive. In the lobby the women threw off their snow-flecked furs and held against their shoulders sprays of white lilies. Single blossoms adorned the lapels of the dandies who held tall ... ebony canes with ivory tops in their white-gloved hands.

The magic of the scene, in which the warmth of glamour seemed to melt the coldness of the night, was matched by the magic of the play, which enfolded the audience into a world where the harsh differences between duty and pleasure, respectable family and dark passion, truth and lies, life and fiction, depth and surface, sincerity and insincerity, the serious and the trivial, are all dissolved by the heat of laughter. Everyone loved it. Even the *New York Times*, which had never found it easy to like Wilde, declared his victory in no uncertain terms: "Oscar Wilde may be said to have at last, and by a single stroke, put his enemies under his feet."

The Importance of Being Earnest begins with the familiar terrain of the double life, in which extramarital pleasures are pursued in secret. One protagonist is called Jack when he is in the country, where he lives an exemplary life raising his youthful ward, Cecily Cardew, and Ernest when he comes to the city, where he pursues pleasure, free of the rigors of respectability. The situation of the other protagonist, Algernon Moncrieff, is reversed. In the city he is taxed by family duties, which take the form of social obligations to his Aunt Augusta (Lady Bracknell); the country is the realm of relief for him. Here he roams to find the pleasures that are denied him in London. He invents a sick friend in the country called Bunbury, whom he uses as an excuse to get out of the city:

> Jack: My dear fellow ... Old Mr. Thomas Cardew, who adopted me when I was a little boy, made me in his will guardian to his grand-daughter, Miss Cecily Cardew. Cecily, who addresses me as her uncle from motives of respect that you could not possibly appreciate, lives at my place in the country under the charge of her admirable governess, Miss Prism ... when one is placed in the position of guardian, one has to adopt a very high moral tone on all subjects. It's one's duty to do so. And as a high moral tone can hardly be said to conduce very much to either one's health or one's happiness,

in order to get up to town I have always pretended to have a younger brother of the name of Ernest, who lives in the Albany, and gets into the most dreadful scrapes....

Algernon: ... What you really are is a Bunburyist.... You are one of the most advanced Bunburyists I know.... You have invented a very useful younger brother called Ernest, in order that you may be able to come up to town as often as you like. I have invented an invaluable permanent invalid called Bunbury, in order that I may be able to go down into the country whenever I choose. Bunbury is perfectly invaluable.

In the act that follows, Algernon follows Jack to his country home, posing as the bad brother Ernest, and promptly falls in love with Cecily. Lady Bracknell, Algernon's aunt, has forbidden the marriage of her daughter Gwendolen and Jack on the grounds of his dubious lineage. Jack is an orphan whom Mr. Thomas Cardew found in a handbag at a railway station. "To be born, at any rate bred, in a hand-bag," Lady Bracknell declares, "whether it had handles or not, seems to me to display a contempt for the ordinary decencies of family life that reminds one of the worst excesses of the French Revolution." For all of the fun of Lady Bracknell's remark, the connection she makes between "contempt for the ordinary decencies of family life" and the "worst excesses of the French Revolution" recalls the intense anxiety that Victorian culture felt about deviations from the heterosexual norm of marriage and children. Whether it is adultery, illegitimacy, or the premarital involvements that Algernon and Jack pursue, pleasures that take place outside the family are always potential threats to the security of the status quo.

In retaliation for Lady Bracknell's rejection of him, Jack refuses to allow Cecily to marry Algernon. To make matters worse, both girls insist that they can only love men who are named, as both men claim to be, Ernest. Just as everyone prepares for a life of passionate celibacy, Miss Prism, Cecily's tutor, comes up in the conversation:

> Lady Bracknell (starting): Miss Prism! Did I hear you mention a Miss Prism? ... Is this Miss Prism a female of repellent aspect, remotely connected with education?

Miss Prism then appears before Lady Bracknell:

> Lady Bracknell (in a severe, judicial voice): Prism! ... Where is that baby? ... Twenty-eight years ago, Prism, you left Lord Bracknell's house, Number 104, Upper Grosvenor Street, in charge of a perambulator that contained a baby of the male sex. You never returned. A few weeks later, through the elaborate investigations of the Metropolitan police, the perambulator was discovered at midnight standing by itself in a remote corner of Bayswater. It contained the manuscript of a three-volume novel of more than usually revolting sentimentality. But the baby was not there. Prism! Where is that baby?

Jack is, of course, the missing child, and therefore Algernon is, as he claimed all along, his brother; an investigation reveals that Jack's real name is Ernest, just as he pretended it was:

> Jack: Gwendolen, it is a terrible thing for a man to find out suddenly that all his life he has been speaking nothing but the truth. Can you forgive me?
> Gwendolen: I can. For I feel that you are sure to change.

It is difficult not to read in Wilde's miraculous comedy about the union of duty and pleasure a wishful fantasy about the rec-onciliation of the duties of marriage and the form of extramarital pleasure that was Wilde's in particular. It is difficult not to read *The Importance of Being Earnest* as a utopian day-dream of a world in which shameful pleasures could be made lawful. But the rule forbidding homosexuality is more formi-dable by far than the one that discourages the heterosexual amours of Jack and Algernon. While those passions can be con-summated ultimately in marriage, homosexual ones never can be. What Alfred Douglas called the love that dare not speak its name has no place at the altar.

The situation of the homosexual is more accurately depicted by Mrs. Erlynne in *Lady Windermere's Fan*, as she pleads with her daughter to avoid the scandal of adultery that she brought on herself. In her passionate exhortation, it is hard not to hear Wilde warning himself, and others like him:

> Believe what you choose about me. I am not worth a moment's sorrow. But don't spoil your beautiful young life.... You don't know what it is to fall into the pit, to be despised, mocked, abandoned, sneered at—to be an outcast! to find the door shut against one, to have to creep in by hideous byways, afraid every moment lest the mask should be stripped from one's face, and all the while to hear the laughter, the horrible laughter of the world, a thing more tragic than all the tears the world has ever shed. You don't know what it is. One pays for one's sin, and then pays again, and all one's life one pays. You must never know that.

If the visible recipient of this speech does not know what it is to "be despised, mocked, abandoned, sneered at," surely Wilde himself did. *Lady Windermere's Fan* is melodrama, but even for melodrama, the intensity of the suffering that the speaker of these lines depicts as the consequence of social shame seems excessive; even for melodrama, it seems melodramatic. This passage makes more sense if we see in it, in addition to what is on the surface, a displaced description of the virtually endless feeling of damnation that homosexuals for several centuries have rightly feared as the consequence of public exposure. Like the green carnation that Wilde's coterie wore on the opening night of *Lady Windermere's Fan*, this speech is, at least in part, a "gay thing."

The specter of shame that Mrs. Erlynne envisions as the result of public scandal is one of the most powerful and enduring means by which modern society discourages sexual nonconformity. One need not tell gays and lesbians this. Leaving aside for a moment criminal penalties and overt violence, prosecution by zealots armed with sodomy laws and baseball bats, both Wilde's society and our own police and punish homosexuality through embarrassment, and the fear of embarrassment. Just because this feeling does not involve the loss of life, imprisonment, or bloodshed, does not mean that it is any less powerful a punishment than those meted out by the State or terrorist attack. Everyone—heterosexual, homosexual, or bisexual—who has felt romantic or erotic desire turn to the fear of ridicule knows that the prospect of embarrassment is a powerful source of aversion, one that sometimes keeps us from admitting, even to ourselves, desires that could be called homosexual. Everyone who has ever felt the force of the cliché "I could have died of embarrassment" knows that the specter of shame can be a most potent means of enforcing the rule of heterosexuality.

Shortly after the opening of *The Importance of Being Earnest*, a real-life drama began, one in which Wilde was finally cast in a role much more like that of Mrs. Erlynne than he may have wanted for himself. "My lot has been one of public infamy,"

Wilde declared in *De Profundis*, the long letter he wrote from the prison where he was sent for violation of the Labouchere Amendment. "I used to say that I thought I could bear a real tragedy if it came to me with purple pall and a mask of noble sorrow, but ... the dreadful thing ... was ... tragedy [in] the raiment of comedy." Convicted of homosexuality, Wilde was forced to march in the footsteps of Mrs. Erlynne:

> Everything about my tragedy has been hideous, mean, repellent, lacking in style.... On November 13th, 1895, I was brought down here from London. From two o'clock till half-past two on that day I had to stand on the centre platform of Clapham Junction in convict dress, and handcuffed, for the world to look at. I had been taken out of the hospital ward without a moment's notice being given to me. Of all possible objects I was the most grotesque. When people saw me they laughed. Each train as it came up swelled the audience. Nothing could exceed their amusement. That was, of course, before they knew who I was. As soon as they had been informed they laughed still more. For half an hour I stood there in the grey November rain surrounded by a jeering mob.

Awakened from the dream of *The Importance of Being Earnest*, Wilde discovered again that certain passions, including his own, could never be reconciled to the demands of family duty and the laws of the State.

chapter ■
SIX

The Fall

You don't know what it is to fall into the pit, to be despised, mocked, abandoned, sneered at—to be an outcast! To find the door shut against one, to have to creep in by hideous byways, afraid every moment lest the mask should be stripped from one's face, and all the while hear the laughter, the horrible laughter of the world, a thing more tragic than all tears the world has ever shed.

—from *Lady Windermere's Fan*

THE ROAD TO READING GAOL began in 1891, when Wilde fell head over heels for a beautiful, self-centered aristocrat named Lord Alfred Douglas. In the minds of many, including his own, this last chapter of Wilde's life doubled as a literary narrative. For some who knew Wilde, and for some who have written of him, the story of his disastrous love for Douglas was a replay of the legend that Homer tells of the bloody and ruinous war between the Trojans and the Greeks. In the Wilde version of the story, the part of Helen of Troy, whose elopement with Paris started the war, is played by Douglas. Commenting on Douglas's later efforts to revise history and deny that he and Wilde were ever lovers, Richard Ellmann, in his learned and compassionate biography of Wilde, wryly recalls that "Homer shows how Helen, back from Troy, blamed Venus for the elopement with Paris, and insisted that she had always longed to be back with her husband."

For Wilde himself, the affair with Douglas, and the ruin that ensued from it, had the earmarks of another classical narrative: it was an exercise in the Greek art of Tragedy: "I discern in all our relations," Wilde wrote to the beautiful young man he called Bosie, "not destiny, merely, but Doom." "I love him as I always did, with a sense of tragedy and ruin," he declared to Robert Ross years later; "My life cannot be patched up. There is a doom on it." Whatever its classical antecedents, the love affair between Wilde and Douglas had all the sensationalism and scriptedness of any good melodrama—with one difference: at the end of the night, the actors in a melodrama go home. But Wilde was ruined in earnest—humiliated, bankrupted, imprisoned, exiled, and condemned to an early death by a State and a Society that found it impossible to tolerate the idea of men in bed together.

The basic plot of Wilde's destruction is as well known as Homer's story, or any Greek tragedy: an ever more public affair with Douglas led to threats and accusations from the young man's violent and eccentric father, the Marquess of Queensberry. Goaded by Douglas, by his own delusions of immunity, and by a disinclination to turn and run, Wilde sued the father for libel. "Blindly I staggered," Wilde wrote, "as an oxen into the shambles." A string of male prostitutes as well as Wilde's own writings were corralled into the courtroom and presented as evidence to confirm Queensberry's accusations. Queensberry was exonerated, and Wilde in turn prosecuted, convicted, and sentenced to two years of hard labor under the terms of the Labouchere Amendment. While he was in prison, Wilde's long-suffering wife divorced him, changing her own name as well as that of their sons. After prison, stripped of his fortune, his glory, and his family, almost friendless, broken in body and spirit, Wilde lived out his three remaining years on the Continent in poverty, obscurity, and shame.

All that was in the future when, in the spring of 1892, he fell in love with Lord Alfred Douglas, whose "rose-leaf lips" were, in Wilde's eyes, "made no less for music of song than for madness of kisses." These words were part of the praise that Wilde showered on a poem Douglas had written in one of his frequent outbursts of extravagant affection:

My own Boy,

Your sonnet is quite lovely and it is a marvel that those red rose-leaf lips are made no less for music of song than for madness of kisses. Your slim gilt soul walks between passion and poetry. I know Hyacinthus, whom Apollo loved so madly was you in Greek days. Why are you alone in London and when do you go to Salisbury? Do go there to cool your hands in the grey twilight of gothic things, and come here whenever you like. It is a lovely place and it only lacks you. But go to Salisbury first.

Always with undying love, yours, Oscar.

The sonnets he wrote were not the only aspect of Alfred Douglas that inspired Wilde to such ecstasies of longing. Wilde's letters are full of love for every part of his "Greek and gracious" form. "You are the divine thing I want," he declared to Douglas, "the thing of grace and beauty." "Dear, dear boy, you are more to me than any one of them has any idea; you are the atmosphere of beauty through which I see life; you are the incarnation of all lovely things," he wrote on another occasion.

"He is quite like a narcissus," Wilde wrote Robert Ross in the summer of 1892, "so white and gold." If, by Wilde's delirious account, Douglas was the most beautiful young man in the world, the youngest son of the Marquess of Queensberry was by all other accounts one of the most difficult: tempestuous, reckless, quick tempered, self-centered, and vindictive. At first just one of the crowd of aspiring young writers and artists from Oxford and Cambridge who surrounded Wilde, Douglas was soon singled out. As Wilde noted in *De Profundis*, their relationship began with a blackmail scandal. In the spring of 1892, Douglas sought Wilde's help with a blackmail threat he had received over an incriminating letter. Wilde sent Douglas to his solicitor, who arranged to hush things up.

As spring turned to summer, Wilde's intimacy with the Oxford undergraduate deepened. By the fall, they were lovers and constant companions. Their exchanges were not limited to gifts, letters, and sonnets. They included as well all sorts of sexual companions. By the end of 1892, Wilde and Douglas had befriended Alfred Taylor, who made his living procuring male hustlers for wealthy patrons, as well as keeping rooms for clients and prostitutes to meet. It was a form of pleasure so dangerous and thrilling that Wilde would later compare it to "feasting with panthers."

Over the course of his affair with Douglas, Wilde became less and less careful about maintaining the secrecy necessary for a homosexual to survive in late Victorian England. His indiscretions were not a matter merely of lavish entertainments for young men of often dubious character and class circumstances. During the first half of the 1890s, Wilde became associated with various literary enterprises that were as explicitly homosexual as the period allowed. He consented to publish something in the *Spirit Lamp*, an Oxford literary journal that Douglas edited, devoted to celebrations and defenses of homosexual love; to another short-lived journal with similar purposes called the *Chameleon* he contributed a miscellany of aphorisms entitled "Phrases and Philosophies for the Use of the Young."

The same issue of the *Chameleon* (only one issue of the journal ever appeared) included a poem by Douglas called "Two Loves," in which what is probably the world's most famous characterization of homosexuality makes its debut. Douglas's poem casts heterosexual and homosexual desire as allegorical figures:

> ... one did joyous seem
> And fair and blooming, and a sweet refrain
> Came from his lips; he sang of pretty maids
> And joyous love of comely girl and boy....
> But he that was his comrade walked aside;
> He was full sad and sweet, and his large eyes
> Were strange with wondrous brightness, staring wide
> With gazing; and he sighed with many sighs
> That moved me, and his cheeks were wan and white
> ... I cried, "Sweet youth,
> Tell me why, sad sighing, thou dost rove
> These pleasant realms
> I pray speak me sooth
> What is thy name?" He said, "My name is Love."
> Then straight the first did turn himself to me

And cried, "He lieth, for his name is Shame,
But I am Love, and I was wont to be
Alone in this fair garden, till he came
Unasked by night; I am true Love, I fill
The hearts of boy and girl with mutual flame."
Then sighing, said the other, "Have thy will,
I am the love that dare not speak its name."

As well as providing a paper trail of evidence that would be used against Wilde at his trials, the *Chameleon* and the *Spirit Lamp* fueled the fury of Douglas's father against the literary celebrity who was, in his eyes, corrupting his son. Apart from codifying the rules for amateur boxing that remain in force to this day, the Marquess of Queensberry was mostly known in his own time as a truculent and perhaps more than slightly insane crackpot. However much an outcast, though, Queensberry carried the banner of outraged Family Values in triumph against the man whom many defenders of a repressive standard of morality had come to think of as enemy number one.

Wilde was no doubt right when, in *De Profundis*, he characterized himself as a pawn in an ongoing war between father and son. The two had despised one another for years. One letter, in which Queensberry declared that he had divorced Douglas's mother because he was so horrified by the children that she spawned, especially Alfred himself, was a typical communication between father and son. Lady Queensberry also became alarmed by the affair. "If Mr. Wilde has acted, as I am convinced he has, the part of a Lord Henry Wotton to you, I could have never felt differently towards him than I do, as the murderer of your soul."

Nonetheless, Wilde's charm was capable of exercising its effects even on his most resolute enemy. On April 1, 1894, the Marquess of Queensberry came upon Wilde and Alfred

Douglas at a café and, at their invitation, joined them. "I don't wonder you are so fond of him," he wrote his son later that day, "he is a wonderful man." Later the same day, though, he wrote Douglas again:

> Your intimacy with this man Wilde ... must either cease or I will disown you and stop all money supplies. I am not going to try to analyze this intimacy and I make no charge; but to my mind to pose as a thing is as bad as to be it. With my own eyes I saw you both in the most loathsome and disgusting relationship as expressed by your manner and expression. Never in my experience have I ever seen such a sight as that in your horrible features. No wonder people are talking as they are. Also, I now hear on good authority, but this may be false, that his wife is petitioning to divorce him for sodomy and other crimes. Is this true, or do you not know of it? If I thought the actual thing was true and it became public property, I should be quite justified in shooting him at sight.... Your disgusted so-called father, Queensberry

The next day, Douglas responded with a famous telegraph: "WHAT A FUNNY LITTLE MAN YOU ARE." Letters followed telegrams, and the hostility between Douglas and his father escalated. Queensberry stormed into Wilde's house, and an argument ensued, in which threats of beating and shooting were exchanged.

In the midst of all this melodrama, Wilde was at work writing what many consider the best comedy of the century. For all its miraculous distance from the growing pressure of scandal that no doubt occupied Wilde during the time it was written, *The Importance of Being Earnest* shows signs of the strain of a double life on the verge of breaking down. Wilde's fears for his own life may well have been on his mind when, early in the play, Jack is exposed by means of a misplaced cigarette case:

> Algernon: ... [T]his isn't your cigarette case. This cigarette case is a present from some one of the name of Cecily, and you said you didn't know anyone of that name.
>
> Jack: Well, if you want to know, Cecily happens to be my aunt.
>
> Algernon: Your aunt!
>
> Jack: Yes. Charming old lady she is, too. Lives at Tunbridge Wells. Just give it back to me, Algy.
>
> Algernon: But why does she call herself little Cecily if she is your aunt and lives at Tunbridge Wells? [Reading.] "From little Cecily with her fondest love."
>
> Jack: My dear fellow, what on earth is there in that? Some aunts are tall, some aunts are not tall. That is a matter that surely an aunt may be allowed to decide for herself. You seem to think that every aunt should be exactly like your aunt! That is absurd! For Heaven's sake give me back my cigarette case.
>
> Algernon: Yes. But why does your aunt call you her uncle? "From little Cecily, with her fondest love to her dear Uncle Jack." There is no objection, I admit, to an aunt being a small aunt, but why an aunt, no matter what her size may be, should call her own nephew her uncle, I can't quite make out. Besides, your name isn't Jack at all; it is Ernest.
>
> Jack: It isn't Ernest; it's Jack.
>
> Algernon: You have always told me it was Ernest. I have introduced you to every one as Ernest. You answer to the name of Ernest. You look as if your name was Ernest. You are the most earnest-looking person I ever saw in my life. It is perfectly absurd your saying that your name isn't Ernest. It's on your cards. Here is one of them. [Taking it from case.]

"Mr. Ernest Worthing, B.4, The Albany." I'll keep this as a proof that your name is Ernest if ever you attempt to deny it to me, or to Gwendolen, or to any one else. [Puts the card in his pocket.]

Jack: Well, my name is Ernest in town and Jack in the country, and the cigarette case was given to me in the country....

Algernon: ... Now go on! Tell me the whole thing. I may mention that I have always suspected you of being a confirmed and secret Bunburyist; and I am quite sure of it now.

Algernon's interrogation of Jack sounds like a comic version of prosecution counsel seeking to expose the double life of a homosexual defendant, right down to the code terms that law and science used to describe this "gross indecency" ("confirmed and secret," "an advanced case"). This is no mere coincidence: a misplaced cigarette case had nearly trapped Douglas in a police dragnet the year before *The Importance of Being Earnest* appeared on stage. Another misplaced cigarette case inscribed for one of the "rent boys" Wilde patronized was introduced at his trial as evidence against him a few months later.

More generally, the fragility of a double life exposed by something as trivial as a cigarette case recalls the tenuousness of the secret existence that was the lot of men like Wilde. The specter of misplaced cigarette cases, telltale stains, and slips of a tongue menaced the survival of homosexuals such as Wilde. Jack's exposure in *The Importance of Being Earnest* tells in a comic vein a cautionary tale that filled the late Victorian homosexual with fear: one false move, one trivial error, and the consequence is scandal and ruin.

Thus the dread of being caught in the act of balancing a life of respectability with the pursuit of dubious, even illegal pleasures bleeds through the light heart of *The Importance of Being*

Earnest. Sequestered in a text that seems about as serious as a "Bewitched" episode is the hint of a grave fear that defined, and for many, continues to define, the life of a homosexual. The anxiety that haunts what many consider to be the funniest play ever written is an instance of the insistent pain that for Wilde pervades all literature that matters, what in "The Decay of Lying" he calls the "grief I remember when I laugh."

In *The Importance of Being Earnest,* the two parts of the double life are reconciled: The woman that Ernest romances in the city becomes the respectable wife he can have in the country; the woman that Algernon adores in the country becomes his acceptable city bride. But Wilde himself had no such luck. The disastrous undoing of his own double life approached a climax in early 1895, when Queensberry delivered a card at the Albemarle Club addressed to "Oscar Wilde, posing as a somdomite" [sic]. Queensberry had already sought to make a scene at the opening of *The Importance of Being Earnest,* but Wilde, apprised of the plan in advance, arranged for police to prevent Queensberry from entering the theater. But the confrontation had only been deferred; with the card, the duel had begun.

Whatever Wilde's own doubts, Douglas would hear of no course of action but to prosecute his father for libel. Queried by his lawyer about the truth of Queensberry's charge, Wilde and Douglas simply lied. As usual, Wilde's own vivid account of events is camera ready: "What is loathsome to me is the memory of interminable visits paid by me to the solicitor Humphreys, in your company, when in the ghastly glare of a bleak room you and I would sit with serious faces telling serious lies to a bald man till I really groaned and yawned with ennui."

To defend himself against Wilde's charge, Queensberry retained Edward Carson, Wilde's classmate at Trinity College, who went to court with three lines of argument. First, Wilde's literary works, and in particular, *The Picture of Dorian Gray*, were offered to support Queensberry's charge. Second, his letters to Alfred Douglas were also entered as evidence. Third, some of the men with whom Wilde and Douglas had been involved were rounded up by detectives and terrorized into testifying against him.

In court, Carson zeroed in on Wilde's private correspondence with Douglas. Most important was the letter in which Wilde had written that Douglas's "lips" were "made no less for music of song than for madness of kisses." Douglas had carelessly left the letter in a suit of clothes he had given to a hustler who sought to blackmail Wilde with it. When at the trial he was called upon to describe his exchange with the hustler over the letter, Wilde cast it as a work of art and therefore, according to an argument upon which he had relied all his life, immune from prosecution:

> I said "I suppose you have come about my beautiful letter to Lord Alfred Douglas. If you had not been so foolish as to send a copy of it to Mr. Beerbohm Tree I would gladly have paid you a very large sum of money for the letter as I consider it to be a work of art." He said "a very curious construction can be put on that letter." I said in reply "art is rarely intelligible to the criminal classes." He said "a man has offered me sixty pounds for it." I said to him, "if you take my advice you will go to that man and sell my letter to him for sixty pounds. I myself have never received so large a sum for any prose work of that length, but I am glad to find that there is someone in England who considers a letter of mine worth sixty pounds."

Wilde acknowledged that he had given the man 15 pounds, but to strengthen his claim for the aesthetic value of the letter, he explained that he had arranged for a friend to turn it into a sonnet. His lawyer led Wilde to speak of the poem:

> Clarke: As a matter of fact, the letter was the basis of a French poem that was published in the Spirit Lamp.
> Wilde: Yes.
> Clarke: It is signed Pierre Louîs. Is that the nom de plume of a friend of yours?
> Wilde: Yes—a young French poet of great distinction, a friend of mine who has lived in England.

Wilde may have briefly triumphed here, but disaster followed. In a decisive exchange with Carson, Wilde was asked about a young servant at Oxford named Walter Grainger. "Did you ever kiss him?" Wilde's old classmate wanted to know. "Oh, dear no," Wilde answered in a lapse of thought no larger than a misplaced cigarette case: "He was a peculiarly plain boy. He was unfortunately extremely ugly. I pitied him for it." Carson wasted no time coming in for the kill:

> Carson: Was that the reason why you did not kiss him?
> Wilde: Oh, Mr. Carson you are impertinent and insolent.
> Carson: Why, Sir, did you mention that this boy was extremely ugly?
> Wilde: For this reason. If I were asked why I did not kiss a doormat, I should say because I do not like to kiss doormats. I do not know why I mentioned why he was ugly except that I was stung by the insolent question you put to me and the way you have insulted me through this hearing. Am I to be cross examined because I do not like it?

Wilde was doomed. Even without his remarkable admission about what had kept him from kissing Walter Grainger, the money he paid for the letter that Douglas had left in a suit of clothes, combined with the testimony of the rent boys, sealed the case of the defense. Wilde's counsel had little choice but to withdraw the libel charge.

Many have wondered what prompted Wilde to take on Queensberry when he must have known that he was extraordinarily susceptible to exposure. Many have wondered why he submitted himself to the risk he clearly recognized beforehand, a risk immediately realized when, before the sun set on the first trial, the state turned around and initiated criminal proceedings against him for violations of the 1885 law against homosexuality. Those who attempt to cast the decision to fight Queensberry as an act of war against an intolerant regime must face the fact that Wilde denied the charge the State brought against him rather than defy their right to make it; efforts to make Wilde an early hero in the struggle for homosexual liberation must take account of the fact that he asserted his innocence of the "crime" of which he stood accused rather than suggesting that homosexuality might be no crime at all.

As much as anything else, Wilde was probably propelled by a conviction that he deserved the aristocratic immunity that others around him were granted as a matter of course. Lord Alfred Douglas was never prosecuted, and notwithstanding a challenge on the part of the foreman of the jury at the first of the criminal trials against Wilde, there was never really any question that he would be. Wilde no doubt felt that his prestige rendered him eligible to profit from the double standard that prosecuted some for sodomy, while, in other cases, looking the other way. Nevertheless, if he was inspired to face Queensberry by a spirit of elitism, Wilde was prompted as well by a lifelong habit of refusing to retreat from bullies, an admirable trait even when accompanied, as in his case, by a sense that he deserved special protection from them.

It would have been possible for Wilde to flee from England in time to escape prosecution on indecent acts charges, but again he preferred not to flee the enemy. "I shall stay and do my sentence whatever it is," he declared to Ross. On April 6, 1895, the other shoe dropped. Two detectives came to his rooms: "We have a warrant here, Mr. Wilde, for your arrest on a charge of committing indecent acts." "With what a crash this fell!" Wilde exclaimed. The Lord of London dinner tables was now a pariah: old friends shunned him; his name was removed from the programs for *An Ideal Husband* and *The Importance of Being Earnest*, and soon after, the plays were suspended altogether; his mother succumbed to a sickness of shame from which she never recovered.

Pretrial witnesses against Wilde included the rent boys that had testified against him earlier during the libel proceedings, as well as employees of the Savoy Hotel where he and Douglas had often stayed. One housekeeper testified that she had discovered fecal stains on Wilde's bed sheets; other employees swore they saw men in Wilde's bed.

At the trial itself, Wilde was again asked about his association with the *Chameleon*. What, the prosecutor asked, referring to Douglas's poem, is "the love that dare not speak its name?" Backed against the wall, Wilde, in a fever of passion, let forth a fire of eloquence whose heat we can feel a hundred years later:

The love that dare not speak its name in this century is such a great affection of an older for a younger man as there was between David and Jonathan, such as Plato made the very basis of his philosophy, and such as you find in the sonnets of Michelangelo and Shakespeare. It is that deep spiritual affection that is as pure as it is perfect. It dictates and pervades great works of art like those of Shakespeare and Michelangelo, and those two letters of mine such as they are.

It is in this century so much misunderstood that it may be described as the love that dare not speak its name. And on account of it I am placed where I am now. It is beautiful, it is noble, it is fine. It is the noblest form of affection. There is nothing unnatural about it. It is intellectual, and it repeatedly exists between an elder and a younger man, when the elder man has intellect, and the younger man has all the joy, hope and glamour of life before him. That it should be so the world does not understand. The world mocks at it and sometimes puts one in the pillory for it.

The jury was unable to reach a verdict, and a third trial was ordered. Wilde was finally released on bail, despite the reluctance of the judge.

Harassed and ill, unable to find a hotel that would accommodate him, Wilde was eventually taken in by Ada and Ernest Leverson. Some of his other friends stood by him as well. William Butler Yeats, the Irish poet who had learned much from Wilde, and who would be haunted by the sorrows of his countryman for the rest of his life, brought letters of sympathy and support from the homeland. "He was the unfinished sketch of a great man," Yeats declared years later, "and showed much courage amid the collapse of his fortunes." A plan was devised to help Wilde escape England before he could be convicted, but Wilde had no interest in running away. "A yacht and a very large sum of money was placed at his disposal and all settled for his flight but he refused to go," Yeats reported. "He says he will stand it out and face the worst and no matter how it turns out work on. He will not go down ... or drink, or take poison."

This time, the prosecution presented its case without a hitch. When, after a few hours, the jury returned with a minor question about evidence involving one of the charges, the prosecution counsel exclaimed to Wilde's counsel: "You'll dine your man in Paris tomorrow!" But the lawyer, an old pro, shook his head sadly. He knew better: a few minutes later, the jury returned again, ready with their verdict. Of all the charges against him, except for one, the defendant was found guilty. For the crime of indiscretion, Oscar Fingal O'Flahertie Wills Wilde fell from the stars.

Wilde was first sent to Pentonville Prison, where he began a "black, loathsome life" that was to destroy him body and soul. In addition to the punitive and senseless labor that the prisoners were compelled to perform, there were other torments as well: "Every prisoner," Wilde noted later, "suffers from hunger."

Wilde's Incarceration

Still used as a prison today, Pentonville prison, Wilde's first location of incarceration, was constructed between the years 1840 and 1842 and modeled on Jeremy Bentham's panopticon design. Bentham's design was used in numerous prisons around the country and consisted of a central hall with radiating wings. Originally built to hold 520 prisoners, each prisoner in his own cell, the conditions at Pentonville were thought to be considerably better than at the infamous Newgate prison.

After Pentonville, Wilde was transferred to Wandsworth prison. Wandsworth was also built on the panopticon model, and was designed to house 700 prisoners. Unlike Pentonville, each cell was equipped with its own toilet, but these were eventually removed in order to make room for more prisoners.

Built in 1844, Reading prison was where Wilde spent the remainder of his incarceration. The prison was designed by Sir Gilbert T. Scott and looked much like a castle with towers and turrets on the outer wall. Here Wilde was allowed to have pens and paper, and it was here that he composed *De Profundis*. After his release he wrote his famous poem *The Ballad of Reading Gaol*.

Access to lavatories was restricted to one hour a day, and the buckets that the prisoners were forced to use at all other times overflowed with the diarrhea that the prison food invariably induced.

His life in prison improved somewhat when he was transferred from Pentonville to Wandsworth and finally to Reading Prison, where he was given paper and pens and allowed to write. With these materials, Wilde composed the long letter to Alfred Douglas that was later entitled *De Profundis*. Wilde's letter, which did not appear in uncensored and corrected form until 1960, begins by listing his grievances against Douglas. In Wilde's eyes, Douglas's greatest outrage was his failure to write him in prison:

> Even people who had not known me personally, hearing what ... sorrow had come into my broken life, wrote to ask that some expression of their condolence should be conveyed to me. You alone stood aloof, sent me no message, and wrote me no letter. Of such actions, it is best to say what Virgil says to Dante of those whose lives have been barren in noble impulse and shallow of intention: "*Non ragioniam di lor, ma guardia, e pass*" ("Let us not speak of them, but look, and pass on").

Dante's sentence of silence must have had a familiar ring to the man for whom the letter was written, the man who had called homosexual passion "the love that dare not speak its name." "*Non ragioniam di lor, ma guardia, e pass*" ("Let us not speak of them, but look, and pass on") sounds like a paraphrase of the formula that Wilde's age, and others as well, applied to such passion; "*Non ragioniam di lor, ma guardia, e pass*" sounds like an Italian version of the Latin phrase that the English had rendered as "a crime so horrible that it is not to be mentioned amongst Christians." Even from prison, whether consciously or not, Wilde was busy working his talent for insurrectionary rhetorical cunning: by calling Douglas's refusal to perform the task of a loyal friend a matter to be passed over in silence, Wilde transferred the shame that society reserved for him, and others like him, to a different infraction altogether. What should be passed over in silence, Wilde seems to say, is not the form of love that landed him in prison, but rather the failure of a lover or a friend to perform the duties of the heart.

But if Wilde's letter succeeds in turning one of society's slanderous characterizations of homosexuality on its head, it embraces another. Cleaving to a cultural conception of homosexuality no less familiar in the 20th century than it was in the 19th, *De Profundis* finds in "the love that dare not speak its name" a lethal fate, a drive toward death. In his love for Douglas, Wilde saw

> not destiny, merely, but Doom: doom that walks always swiftly, because she goes to the shedding of blood.... In every little circumstance in which the ways of our lives met; in every point of great or seemingly trivial import in which you came to me for pleasure or for help; in the small chances, the slight accidents that look in their relation to life to be no more than the dust that dances in a beam, or the leaf that flutters from a tree, Ruin followed, like the echo of a bitter cry, or the shadow that hunts with the beast of prey.

"I dare say that what I've done is fatal," Wilde confided to Ross in a letter about his love for Douglas, "but it had to be done."

The fatal shadow that Wilde traces in his love for Douglas haunts his vision of all homosexual passion in *De Profundis*; it hovers, for example, over the thrill of the panther feast:

People thought it dreadful of me to have entertained ... the evil things of life, and to have pleasure in their company ... it was like feasting with panthers. The danger was half the excitement. I used to feel as the snake charmer must feel who lures the cobra to stir from the painted cloth or reed basket that holds it, and makes it spread its hood at his bidding, and sway to and fro in the air as the plant sways restfully in the stream. They were to me the brightest of gilded snakes. Their poison was part of their perfection.

By calling *all* homosexual passions, and not just his catastrophic affair with Douglas, a kind of death wish, Wilde ratified a cultural myth that extends from his own age well into ours. To point out the ongoing effects of the myth of gay doom, we need go no further than the persistent apprehension, in our own time, of the illnesses associated with the Human Immunodeficiency Virus (HIV) as a "gay disease," more than a decade after scientists have refuted it. The image of homosexual doom that wafts through the pages of *De Profundis* reappears in popular accounts that depict gay men as the very face of AIDS. The disastrous consequences of this error for homosexuals and heterosexuals alike make the task of understanding and resisting the legacy of this late Victorian ideology a matter of grave urgency. That the western world's most famous victim of homophobia himself confused his desires with Doom suggests that this urgent task of understanding and resistance is not easy.

Released from prison on May 19, 1897, Wilde returned to the home of his loyal friends, the Leversons. Ada Leverson remembered "the dignity of a king returning from exile. He came in talking, laughing, smoking a cigarette with waved hair and a flower in his buttonhole." But Wilde was a broken man, less a king returning from exile than an outcast compelled to enter it. There was no question of his living in England. As soon as he was able, Wilde left the country that had been his home for most of his life, to spend the few years that remained for him in France.

There, he intended to write a new play, *Pharaoh*, and to complete an old one, *A Florentine Tragedy*. But like most of his plans for new projects, neither of these came to anything. All that he succeeded in writing was the saddest of all his poems, *The Ballad of Reading Gaol*, the story of a man whose execution for the murder of his wife Wilde had witnessed:

> The man had killed the thing he loved,
> And so he had to die.
>
> Yet each man kills the thing he loves,
> By each let this be heard,
>
> Some do it with a bitter look,
> Some with a flattering word,
> The coward does it with a kiss,
> The brave man with a sword!

Alfred Douglas returned to Wilde, only to leave again: neither really had his heart in the affair anymore. Sporadically generous, the now wealthy Douglas resented the idea that Wilde had any claim on his fortune or his loyalty. Wilde's estranged wife died the year after his release from prison; his mother had died the year before. Poverty forced him to practice a genteel form of panhandling: the last letters of one of the 19th century's most astonishing writers are filled with wheedling requests for small sums of money; the last accounts of the most luminous personality of the age describe a man forced to beg for cash. Nellie Melba, an opera singer who knew Wilde at the height of his glory, was approached one day in Paris by a disheveled man whom she did not recognize at first. "Madame Melba," he said, "you don't know who I am. I'm Oscar Wilde, and I'm going to do a terrible thing. I'm going to ask you for money."

During his last years, Wilde was more candid about his homosexuality than he ever had been before, perhaps because there was nothing left for him to lose: "A patriot imprisoned for loving his country loves his country. And a poet imprisoned for loving boys loves boys." Ravaged by prison, poverty, and despair, Oscar Wilde died on November 30, 1900, at the age of 46. His grave is inscribed with words from the Book of Job: "Verbis meus adere nihil audebant et super illos stillebat eloquium meum" (To my words they dared add nothing, and my speech fell upon them).

seven

The Critical Response

[T]here is only one thing in the world worse than being talked about, and that is not being talked about."
                                   —*The Picture of Dorian Gray*

OSCAR WILDE DIED IN 1900, the same year as Nietzsche and a year before Queen Victoria. He was a controversial and well-known figure in late-Victorian England, an era that embraced values of progress, technology, individualism, and morality with a high seriousness. Toward the end of the century, however, also known as the Gay Nineties, Victorian values were beginning to wane, and Victorians were questioning their moral convictions and certainties. Against this setting of the *fin de siècle* rose the figure of Oscar Wilde—celebrated, shining, defiant; and it was from these heights that he fell, toppled by the very society that had once adored him.

From his days at Oxford to his imprisonment, Wilde expressed strong-opinionated views on literature and art, and his celebrated table talk, public demeanor, and provocative plays quickly built his famed reputation. It was Wilde's belief that life should strive to imitate art in all its beauty and sensuality, and that society's moral values should not impede this experience. In both his writing and his personal life, Wilde embraced Walter Pater's advice to "burn always with this hard gemlike flame," and promoted the freedom of self-expression. Thus, near the end of the 19th century, as Oscar Wilde's famous plays unmasked the superficiality of London society, his arrest for "acts of gross indecency," also brought homosexuality into the public arena. Time has proven that Wilde will always be remembered for both his writing and his life, in which, "[f]rom out twentieth-century vantage point ... the name Oscar Wilde virtually means 'homosexual.'"

Before he established himself as a notable writer, Oscar Wilde delighted, and taunted, Victorian England with his celebrated talk, winning both admiration and scorn. His witty remarks and exaggerated anecdotes at the dinner table, along with his foppish affections, quickly earned him a place among London's high society. Yeats called him an "excellent talker" and

Shaw agreed he was the "best English-speaking talker of whom we have record in his time." To the public, he was a witty raconteur, a symbolic leader of Aesthetic movement, and a flamboyant dandy who moved in England's most fashionable circles. Yet, under this theatrical performance existed a bright young man from Ireland with a driving ambition to become a famous writer.

Ironically, Wilde was already a well-known society figure before his first book of poems appeared in 1881. The book received mixed reviews, and today his early poetry is typically dismissed: "Wilde began as a poet, and alas was and always remained quite a bad poet," asserts the scholar Harold Bloom. Wilde's poems failed to yield any sort of literary notoriety, or income, as Richard Aldington points out: "Wilde's poems were published and went into several editions—of two hundred copies each. His sayings were repeated. He was constantly caricatured in *Punch*. But he remained poor and extravagant."

Although by age 30 Wilde was already known throughout Europe for the quotable witticisms that peppered his writing and speech, he wanted to win respect as a writer. Then, in 1890, he published his important work of criticism, "The Critic as Artist," followed by the controversial novel *The Picture of Dorian Gray*. The subject matter offended many critics. A particularly scathing review in the *Daily Chronicle* called the novel "unclean," and a "poisonous book ... with odours of moral and poisonous putrefaction," the reviewer pointing out the "effeminate frivolity" without directly mentioning the homoerotic elements. By now, it has become nearly impossible to read *Dorian Gray* without noting the homoeroticism; however, in Victorian England, for this kind of dialogue—at least not yet. Perhaps sensing the novel would be deemed immoral, Wilde defended himself in the preface: "There is no such thing as a moral or an immoral book. Books are well written or badly written. That is all."

Wilde reached the height of his success in the early 1890s, which was also when Wilde met Lord Alfred Douglas and subsequently became less careful in hiding his romantic and sexual liaisons with men. After the publication of *Dorian Gray*, Wilde turned to theater, and in the next three years, he solidified his reputation as one of the foremost writers of his time with plays such as *Lady Windermere's Fan* and *A Woman of No Importance*, plays that had broad appeal and received enthusiastic reviews. The public delighted in Wilde's satirization of Victorian values, his undermining of middle-class society's obsession with seriousness and respectability. Wilde's plays filled a void, explains

Popularity

At the end of the 19th century, Oscar Wilde's wildly popular plays brought him fame, and helped to establish him as one of England's most eminent playwrights. Today, Wilde's work, internationally known, still delights audiences. Although the plays are set in an the Victorian era, they have stood the test of time as provocative, witty comedies, relevant to contemporary life. Wilde's plays are performed regularly in New York and London, and in various theaters, from traditional to experimental, across the world. Furthermore, *The Importance of Being Earnest* (2002) and *An Ideal Husband* (2000) were both adapted for the screen, and starred such well-known actors as Rupert Everett, Julianne Moore, Cate Blanchett, and Colin Firth. A feature film about Wilde's life, with Stephen Fry, Jude Law, and Vanessa Redgrave, appeared in 1997, and Wilde's only novel, *The Picture of Dorian Gray*, was also made into a movie in 1945, starring George Sanders, Donna Reed, and Angela Landsbury.

the contemporary writer Peter Ackroyd: "In Wilde's lifetime the end of 'Victorianism' (and all that it had come to represent) was in sight, but nothing had come to take its place: it was a time of spiritual, moral, social, and artistic chaos, when even the most formidable conventions and the firmest convictions began to crumble, to slide and eventually to dissolve ... It happened to be Wilde who defined both the conscience and the consciousness of the artists at a time when all other values were thrown into doubt."

Although not all Victorians admired Wilde's work—Henry James, for example, remarked that in *Lady Windermere's Fan*, "There is of course absolutely no characterization and all the people talk equally strained Oscar"—many notable critics and writers praised Wilde. In response to *An Ideal Husband*, playwright Bernard Shaw wrote, "In a certain sense Mr Wilde is to me our only thorough playwright. He plays with everything: with wit, with philosophy, with drama, with actors and audience, with the whole theatre."

Oscar Wilde was already the most quotable personality in the 1890s, and with the publication of his criticism, coupled with the success of his plays, he quickly rose as one of England's premier writers and thinkers. However, Wilde's success quickly unraveled. After the sensational trials in 1895, and at the peak of his career, Wilde lost everything: freedom, family, friends, money, career, and hope. Theaters showing Wilde's plays deleted his name from their programs, his name was dropped from England's fashionable circles, and newspapers proclaimed that Wilde should be erased from memory. In his lifetime, there would be no further West End productions of his plays. When Wilde was released from prison after two years, most of his friends abandoned him. As an Irishman and a homosexual, Oscar Wilde, in spite of his fame, always remained an outsider in British society. Ironically, the same Victorian values and hypocrisies that he mocked on stage—which had once delighted audiences—were what destroyed him in the end.

Oscar Wilde, persecuted and scorned for his homosexuality, was left a broken man. After his imprisonment, he never regained his confidence, and the rehabilitation of his literary reputation did not occur until long after his death in 1900. Productions of his plays began to appear again after his death; however, the real reason for his disappearance from England's literary world was typically not discussed—not until many years later, when the gay and lesbian movement proudly claimed Wilde as an emblem for a hero. At the time of his death, many of Wilde's letters were destroyed by friends, for fear of being implicated of homosexuality, and by the 1920s, his persecution was still usually only alluded to in veiled terms. "At the time the British could not have accepted him otherwise," asserts Wilde's grandson Merlin Holland, "but the approach was sadly misguided, and assessments of his life and literature both suffered in consequence."

For years, before the trials, the public mocked Wilde for his Aesthetic posturing and his dandy mannerisms, and this attention, which Wilde often provoked, enhanced his fame. "Wilde's powers of self-dramatisation were met during his lifetime by multiple dramatisations of his persona in the public domain," points out the critic Anne Varty. "Cartoons, plays, spoof biographies, poems, songs and dances were all composed in response to the elaborately constructed 'self,' which Wilde put on display." However, once Wilde was "outed" as a gay man, he was viciously ostracized. It is important for modern audiences to understand that before the trials, Wilde was not necessarily perceived by his contemporaries as a homosexual, and it was only in the few months leading up to the trials that rumors about him and Bosie began to circulate in London's society circles. In *The Wilde Century*, Alan Sinfield asks, "How did he get away with it?—going around looking and talking the way he did, and putting such characters on the stage. And the answer must be: they didn't see queerness in the way we have come to see it. Our interpretation is retroactive; in fact, Wilde and his writings look queer because our stereotypical notion of male homosexuality derives from Wilde, and our ideas about him."

In the last 20 years, Wilde's work has become quite popular, and his literary reputation has been restored. Wilde's plays on stage have been enormously popular and profitable, and hundreds of books have been written about him. In academia, his work is a popular subject in Victorian studies, gay and lesbian studies, gender studies, and Irish studies. However, the merit of his work still divides scholars: "One part of academia insists that he was simply a passing socio-cultural phenomenon and the author of lightweight popular works; another that he was a modern thinker, bridging two centuries, an astute critic and commentator ...". Many feel similar to Richard Aldington, that "[i]ndeed it is the greatest mistake to rate Wilde too low as a writer. If he had not been an excellent writer he would now be as nearly forgotten as those heroes of resounding British scandals, Charles Parnell and Charles Dilke."

It is nearly impossible to separate Oscar Wilde, the famous writer imprisoned for homosexuality, from his work, which has resulted in both his soaring popularity and also reinforced limiting perspectives, as Louis Menand attests: "The scandalous nature of Wilde's peripeteia contributed to a swift and severe reaction against the view of art he represented; and although his reputation has enjoyed a gradual rehabilitation, he is still sometimes narrowly identified with a kind of amoral aestheticism that many people associate, invidiously or not, with a stereotyped conception of male homosexuality."

One hundred years after his death, Oscar Wilde is remembered as a raconteur, playwright, and cultural critic, and for his startlingly rapid fall from society's graces. At one point, he was one of the most popular personalities and respected playwrights in late-Victorian England, but by the end of his life, he was shunned. However, with his reputation and oeuvre reevaluated, many now regard Wilde as one of the premier English play-wrights. His life and work have inspired a flourishing bibliography of critical studies, biographies, novels, plays, poems, and films.

afterword

Some said my life was a lie but I always knew it to be the truth; for like the truth it was rarely pure and never simple.

—Oscar Wilde

FOR THE BIOGRAPHER, WILDE'S LIFE presents many contradictions, yet also offers a rich palate of material. Early biographies of Wilde were filled with mistakes and speculations, but the release of his collected letters in 1962 helped to clarify many rumors. Still, Wilde, with his biting witticisms, flamboyant wardrobe, and conflicting identities, remains a complicated and provocative subject. Over a hundred years after his death, arguments about his work and personal life flourish: "Biographers now have access to such a wealth of material that Wilde's private and public lives may be picked over like few others'. Paradoxically (what else) this makes Wilde's life more contradictory and complicated than ever."

Oscar Wilde, a prolific literary genius and social critic, reached the peak of this success in the late 19th century England. He left behind a legacy that encompasses both his oeuvre and his life, the two inseparable; he is remembered for his brilliant plays, his reckless personality, his clever epigrams, and for his trials in England, in which he was persecuted for being a homosexual.

Today, his work has grown in popularity and importance. "He is not one of those writers who as the centuries change lose their relevance," attests Richard Ellmann. "Wilde is one of us. His wit is an agent of renewal, as pertinent now as a hundred years ago."

Indeed, Wilde's life has a particular timely relevance. One hundred years ago, Wilde was sentenced to prison for engaging in sexual acts with other men; in other words, he was punished for being gay. Not surprisingly, Oscar Wilde has been embraced by the modern gay and lesbian movement as a martyr and hero. Although it is easy to oversimplify and romanticize Wilde's participation in the struggle for gay and lesbian liberation, we also owe something to Wilde (even if he did proclaim "innocence") for defying social conventions and standing up against intolerance. Wilde lived in a society that viewed homosexuality an abomination, in which the love between two men or two women was reduced to a "love that dare not speak its name." Although today, "coming out" is a common phrase, and "gay issues" appear regularly in pop culture and political platforms, the gay and lesbian struggle against repression is far from over. Just as Wilde's trials once captivated Victorian England, today in twenty-first century America, all eyes are on the trials concerning the legality of gay and lesbian marriage, a controversy that has touched everyone from queer activists to the religious right to the middle-class, middle-America family. Furthermore, in a particularly relevant example, twelve U.S. states, until recently, still had "sodomy laws"—similar to the British law that sentenced Oscar Wilde to prison. But on November 18, 2003, the Supreme Court struck down a sodomy law in Texas with a six to three decision, reversing a 17-year-old ruling. This momentous court ruling, which puts an end to the classification of homosexuality as "deviant sex," will help provide legal protection for gays and lesbians, and potentially achieve more mainstream acceptance and visibility.

During the era of the Victorians, the trials of Oscar Wilde heavily influenced the public perception of homosexuality. At the time, "his case was already so well known that it had significantly altered the shape of the Victorian sexual imagination," points out critic Ed Cohen. "For, by the time of his conviction, not only had Wilde been confirmed as the sexual deviant for the late nineteenth century, but he had become the paradigmatic example of an emerging public definition of a new "type" of male sexual actor: "the homosexual." Wilde's trials helped to bring the homosexual into the public sphere, yet, at the same time, they heightened society's paranoia about homosexuality, driving gay men and lesbians back into the closet for decades. The critic Alan Sinfield adds, "For us, it is hard to regard Wilde as other than the apogee of gay experience and expression, because that is the position we have accorded him in our cultures ... But Wilde's typicality is after-the-effect ... the trials helped to produce a major shift in perception of the scope of the same-sex passion." Although Wilde was persecuted—and symbolically destroyed—by the trials, he also brought homosexuality into the public sphere, and thus, contributed—although not by choice—to the long fight for gay and lesbian visibility.

Although Oscar Wilde is often memorialized for his startlingly rapid fall from society's graces, his homosexuality, and the famous criminal trials that sentenced him to two years of hard labor for "acts of gross indecency;" it is his timeless, provocative writing that has established him as one of England's most important authors. As Richard Ellmann eloquently argues, Wilde's work is as relevant today as it was during his lifetime:

> His work survived as he claimed it would. We inherit his struggle to achieve supreme fictions in art, to associate art with social change, to bring together individual and social impulse, to save what is eccentric and singular from being sanitized and standardized, to replace a morality of severity by one of sympathy. He belongs to our world more than to Victoria's. Now, beyond the reach of scandal, his best writings validated by time, he comes before us still, a towering figure, laughing and weeping, with parables and paradoxes, so generous, so amusing and so right.

The last few years of Wilde's life were terribly lonely and painful, as he was outcast from society, and his work was neglected and ignored. However, Wilde has not been forgotten.

His grave is inscribed with words from the Book of Job: "Verbis meus adere nihil audebant et super illos stillebat eloquium meum" (To my words they dared add nothing, and my speech fell upon them). A hundred years later, Wilde's words are with us still. Wilde was a conversationalist unmatched in England, a master of style, and one of the greatest writers of his time. The comedy of his paradoxical and aphoristic wit still delights and instructs us; his assertion that the work of the imagination not only receives reality but helps to make it still educates us; the vision he described of a more honest, enlightened, and compassionate world still moves us; the world he foresaw, where dissident desires can live without fear or shame, still provokes us. And, in the story of his fall, as well as of his opposition to the forces of repression that caused it, generations of men and women like Wilde have found inspiration for their own struggle with these forces. Not the least of Wilde's gifts to the future is the help he has bequeathed to a struggle for liberation that will make the pain that he suffered a thing of the past.

WORKS CITED

Ackroyd, Peter. "Oscar Wilde: Comedy as Tragedy." *The New York Times on the Web*. November 1, 1987. *www.nytimes.com/books/ 00/02/06/specials/ackroyd-Wilde.html?oref=login*.

Aldington, Richard and Stanley Weintraub, ed. *The Portable Oscar Wilde*. New York: Penguin Books, 1981.

Beckson, Karl, ed. *Oscar Wilde: The Critical Heritage*. London: Routledge and Kegan Paul, 1970.

Bloom, Harold, ed. *Modern Critical Views: Oscar Wilde*. New York: Chelsea House Publishers, 1985.

Cohen, Ed. *Talk on the Wilde Side: Toward a Genealogy of a Discourse on Male Sexualities*. New York: Routledge, 1993.

Ellmann, Richard. *Oscar Wilde*. New York: Vintage Books, 1987.

———, ed. *Oscar Wilde: A Collection of Critical Essays*. Englewood Cliffs, NJ: Prentice Hall, 1969.

Lacey, Colin. "The Importance of Being Oscar." *Irish Aroad: Daily Irish News*. <*www.irishabroad. com/irish world/irishamericamag/ decjan05/hibernia/speranza.asp*>

Holland, Merlin. "Biography and the Art of Lying." *The Cambridge Companion to Oscar Wilde*. Peter Raby, ed. Cambridge: Cambridge University Press, 1997.

Menand, Louis. "Oscar Wilde." *The Johns Hopkins Guide to Literary Theory & Criticism*. <*www.press.jhu.edu/books/hopkins_ guide_to_literary_theory/oscar_wilde.html*>

"Oscar Wilde's Epitgrammatic Theater." *Reading Wilde, Querying Spaces*. <*www.nyu.edu/library/bobst/research/fales/exhibits/wilde/ 0chamele.htm*>

Sedgwick, Eve Kosofsky. "Some Binarisms (II): Wilde, Nietzsche, and the Sentimental Relations of the Male Body." *Epistemology of the Closet*. Berkeley: University of California Press, 1990.

Sinfield, Alan. *The Wilde Century*. London: Casell, 1994.

Varty, Anne. *A Preface to Oscar Wilde*. London: Addison-Wesley Longman, 1998.

1854	Born Oscar Fingal O'Flahertie Wills Wilde on October 16, in Dublin, Ireland.
1871–74	Attends Trinity College, Dublin; wins Berkeley Gold Medal for Greek.
1874–78	Attends Magdalen College, Oxford; wins "double first" in university degree examinations.
1880	Writes *Vera, or, The Nihilists*.
1881	*Poems* published.
1882	Wilde lectures in the United States and Canada.
1883	Writes *The Duchess of Padua*.
1884	Marries Constance Lloyd.
1888	*The Happy Prince and Other Tales* is published.
1889	"The Portrait of Mr. W.H." appears in Blackwood's.
1890	*The Picture of Dorian Gray* is published in *Lippincott's Monthly Magazine*.
1891	"The Soul of Man Under Socialism" is published in the *Fortnightly Review*; *The Picture of Dorian Gray* appears in book form with various changes; *Intentions* (a collection of essays), *Lord Arthur Savile's Crime and Other Stories*, and *A House of Pomegranates* are also published; Wilde meets Lord Alfred Douglas.
1892	*Lady Windermere's Fan* opens at the St. James's Theatre.
1893	Salome is published simultaneously in English and French; *A Woman of No Importance* opens at the Theatre Royal, Haymarket.
1894	"The Sphinx" is published; the *Chameleon*, containing Wilde's "Phrases and Philosophies for the Use of the Young" appears.
1895	*An Ideal Husband* opens at the Haymarket Theatre; *The Importance of Being Earnest* opens at the St. James's Theatre; Wilde sues the Marquess of Queensberry for libel, after receiving a card from him calling him a

sodomite; trial begins on April 3; Wilde withdraws prosecution, and Queensberry is acquitted on April 5; on the
next day, Wilde is arrested for homosexuality; first criminal trial begins on April 26; jury unable to reach a verdict, and Wilde is released on bail on May 7; on May 20,
second criminal trial begins; Wilde is found guilty and
sentenced to two years imprisonment and hard labor on
May 25.

1897   Chancery court grants Constance Wilde custody of their
sons Cyril and Vyvyan; the children's surname is changed
to Holland; Wilde finishes writing *De Profundis*, released
from prison on May 19.

1898   *The Ballad of Reading Gaol* is published; Constance Wilde
dies.

1900   Wilde dies of meningitis in Paris.

Ravenna (1878)

Vera; or, The Nihilists (1880)

Poems (1881)

The Duchess of Padua: A Tragedy of the XVI Century (1883)

The Happy Prince and Other Tales (1888)

The Picture of Dorian Gray (1891)

Intentions (1891)

Lord Arthur Savile's Crime and Other Stories (1891)

A House of Pomegranates (1891)

Salome (in French) (1893)

Lady Windermere's Fan: A Play about a Good Woman (1893)

Salome, translated by Lord Alfred Douglas; (1894)

"The Sphinx" (1894)

A Woman of No Importance (1894)

Oscariana: Epigrams (1895)

The Soul of Man Under Socialism (1895)

The Ballad of Reading Gaol (1898)

Children in Prison and Other Cruelties of Prison Life (1898)

The Importance of Being Earnest: A Trivial Comedy for Serious People (1899)

An Ideal Husband (1899)

Sebastian Melmoth (1904)

De Profundis (1905)

The Rise of Historical Criticism (1905)

Four Letters Which Were Not Included in the English Edition of De Profundis (1906)

The Suppressed Portion of De Profundis. Edited by Robert Ross (1913)

For Love of the King: A Burmese Masque (1922)

Essays. Edited by Hesketh Pearson (1950)

Letters. Edited by Rupert Hart-Davis (1962)

More Letters. Edited by Rupert Hart-Davis (1985)

Bartlett, Neil. *Who Was the Man?: A Present for Mr. Oscar Wilde.* London: Serpent's Tail, 1988.

Cohen, Ed. *Talk on the Wilde Side: Toward a Genealogy of a Discourse on Male Sexualities.* New York: Routledge, 1993.

Dollimore, Jonathan. *Sexual Dissidence: Augustine to Wilde, Freud to Foucault.* Oxford: Clarendon Press, 1991.

Ellmann, Richard. *Oscar Wilde.* New York: Vintage Books, 1987.

Gagnier, Regina. *Idylls of the Marketplace: Oscar Wilde and the Victorian Public.* Stanford: Stanford University Press, 1986.

Huysmans, J.K. *Against the Grain.* Translation of the original 1884 edition. New York: Dover Books, 1969.

Hyde, H. Montgomery. *The Trials of Oscar Wilde.* New York: Dover, 1962.

Pater, Walter. *The Renaissance.* 1893. Reprint. Chicago: Pandora Books, 1978.

Sedgwick, Eve Kosofsky. *Between Men: English Literature and Male Homosocial Desire.* New York: Columbia University Press, 1985.

Weeks, Jeffrey. *Coming Out: Homosexual Politics in Britain, from the Nineteenth Century to the Present.* New York: Quartet Books, 1979.

———. *Sex, Politics and Society: The Regulation of Sexuality Since 1800.* New York: Longman, 1981.

Wilde, Oscar. *The Letters of Oscar Wilde.* Edited by Rupert Hart-Davis. New York: Harcourt, Brace & World, 1962.

———. *The Works of Oscar Wilde.* Leicester, England: Blitz Editions, 1990.

Winwar, Frances. *Oscar Wilde and the Yellow Nineties.* New York: Harper & Brothers, 1940.

WEBSITES:

The Oscar Wilde Collection
www.oscarwildecollection.com/

Oscar Wilde Homepage
www.cmgww.com/historic/wilde/

Oscar Wilde: Story in Depth
www.gayhistory.com/rev2/events/wilde.htm

Oscar Wilde – Wikipedia
http://en.wikipedia.org/wiki/Oscar_Wilde

The Picture of Oscar Wilde: A Brief Biography
www.victorianweb.org/authors/wilde/wildebio.html

Reading Wilde, Querying Spaces
www.nyu.edu/library/bobst/research/fales/exhibits/wilde/
0chamele.htm

The Trials of Oscar Wilde
www.law.umkc.edu/faculty/projects/ftrials/wilde/wilde.htm

INDEX

INDEX

INDEX

INDEX

CONTRIBUTORS

JEFF NUNOKAWA is Professor of English at Princeton University and specializes in English literature from 1830 till 1900. He is author of *The Afterlife of Property; Tame Passions of Wilde: Styles of Manageable of Desire*, and various articles discussing nineteenth century literature. His current project is a book whose working title is something like "Eros and Isolation: Getting Away from Others in Nineteenth Century Literature."

AMY SICKELS is a freelance writer living in New York City. She received her MFA in creative writing from Penn State University and she has published short stories, essays, and book reviews in numerous journals, including *Fourth Genre, Kalliope*, and *Literary Review*.

LESLÉA NEWMAN is the author of 50 books including the picture books *Heather Has Two Mommies* and *The Boy Who Cried Fabulous*; the short story collections *A Letter to Harvey Milk* and *Out of the Closet and Nothing to Wear*; the poetry collection *Still Life with Buddy*; the novels *In Every Laugh a Tear* and *Jailbait*; and the writing manual, *Write from the Heart*. She has received many literary awards including Poetry Fellowships from the Massachusetts Artists Fellowship Foundation and the National Endowment for the Arts, the Highlights for Children Fiction Writing Award, the James Baldwin Award for Cultural Achievement, and three Pushcart Prize Nominations. Nine of her books have been Lambda Literary Award finalists.